PAUL, MASTER OF THE SPIRITUAL LIFE

Paul, Master of the spiritual life

CHARLES AUGRAIN, S.S.

VOLUME I

alba house · DIVISION OF THE SOCIETY OF ST. PAUL
STATEN ISLAND, N.Y. 10314

Translated by Sr. M. Paul Purcell, M.A., Dip. Ed.
Copyright The Mercier Press, 1967

Library of Congress Catalog Number: 67-24923

Nihil Obstat:
Jeremiah J. O'Sullivan, D.D.
Censor deputatus

Imprimatur:
† Cornelius
Ep. Corcag & Ross
30th August, 1966

Printed and bound in the U.S.A. by the Pauline Fathers and Brothers of
the Society of St. Paul at Staten Island, New York as a part of their
communications apostolate.

Key

books of the old testament

	Abbr.		Abbr.
Genesis	Gen.	Ecclesiastes . . .	Eccl.
Exodus	Ex.	Wisdom	Wis.
Leviticus	Lev.	Isaias	Is.
Numbers	Num.	Jeremias	Jer.
Deuteronomy . . .	Dt.	Ezechiel	Ez.
Josue	Jos.	Daniel	Dan.
Kings	Kg.	Osee	Os.
Job	Job	Amos	Am.
Psalms	Ps.	Aggeus	Ag.
4 Kings	4 Kg.	Zacharias	Za.

books of the new testament

The Holy Gospel
  according to:
St. Matthew . . . . Mt.
St. Mark . . . . . Mk.
St. Luke . . . . . Lk.
St. John . . . . . Jn.
The Acts
  of the Apostles . . Ac.
The Epistles of St. Paul
  to the:
Romans . . . . Rom.
  I Corinthians . . I Cor.
II Corinthians . . II Cor.
Galatians . . . . . Gal.
Ephesians . . . . Eph.
Philippians . . . Phil.
Colossians . . . . . Col.
  I Thessalonians . . I Th.
II Thessalonians . . II Th.

I Timothy . . . I Tim.
II Timothy . . . II Tim.
Titus . . . . . Tit.
Philemon . . . Phm.
Hebrews . . . Heb.
I St. Peter . . . I Pet.
II St. Peter . . . II Pet.
  I St. John . . . I Jn.
II St. John . . . II Jn.
III St. John . . . III Jn.
The Apocalypse . . Apoc.

Contents

Foreword

To introduce the work 'Paul Maître de Vie Spirituelle' needs none other but Charles Augrain, professor in the famous diocesan seminary, Saint Sulpice, (Paris), founded in 1645 by Jean-Jacques d'Olier, the man who 'did great things for God and the Church,' by spreading a more exact knowledge of Christian principles and the Christian way of life among the society of his time.

To my request for a preface for this translation I received from His Excellency Count Finbar Ryan, D.D., O.P., the Archbishop of Port of Spain, Trinidad, the following gracious reply which will serve to introduce my translation to its readers.

'Thank you for your kind letter with its flattering invitation to write an introduction to your translation of what would seem to be a work of greatest importance for those seeking the perfection of the spiritual life.

It would be indeed a pleasure to say 'Yes'...

Let me congratulate you on your remarkable academic record and on the persistence in the use of the gifts bestowed on you by God... for His glory. My dear sister, to whom you so appreciatively refer was, as you probably know, an ardent believer in the right and duty of women to develop and use their intellectual talents.'

His sister, the late Mary Ryan, M.A., whose student I had the pleasure and privilege of being, was the beloved and revered professor who so kindly, encouragingly and painstakingly guided my early steps in the French Department, University College, Cork.

In presenting this translation I wish to pay a public tribute of homage and respect to her and, through her, to all priests, professors, parents and teachers who like her, perform the daily duty of their state in a similarly conscientious manner, thus guiding youth over those dangerous

inexperienced years of life's rosy morning during which
the foundation of mandhood's fair prime is laid.

Sr. M. Paul Purcell,
St. Maries of the Isle,
Cork, 1966

Introduction

'Every time I read a passage of Paul's *Letters* and recognise his friendly voice, I feel I see him in front of me and hear him talking to me.' Now, who speaks with so much congenial understanding? A Father of the Church, Saint John Chrysostom, who amidst the many cares of his charge as Bishop of Constantinople, used to seek in the *Epistles* of St. Paul, comfort, light, and peace.

Yes, all these the *Epistles* can give us, too; but only on condition that, like Chrysostom, we know them intimately and thoroughly. Certainly, we have a superficial knowledge of them: throughout the liturgical year, readings from the missal give us a few passages from them. But is that enough? Don't we know ourselves that Paul's thought is too deep and too rich to be really accessible in these short extracts? These are but tiny fragments, which are fully understood only by the person who can replace them in their proper setting and explain them by the author's personality. Because we do not know St. Paul's writings thoroughly; because we are not intimate with this exceptional character as radiantly attractive today as ever, we run the risk of losing much of the spiritual nourishment contained in the liturgy.

Therefore, we want to initiate our reader in the knowledge of Paul himself and of his message. Our object is to do so in the most natural way, by following the *Epistles* themselves in their historic order. Thus we will grasp Paul's thought at its very source, in that practical character of his which provides the answer to all questions asked and all problems set by the Christian communities founded by him. Because in his case, theological thought is intimately connected with apostolic action, Paul is certainly one of the most remarkable examples in history of a man of thought who is at the same time a man of action. Founder of Churches, he is also a theologian who constructed a doctri-

11

nal work of capital importance and he could only be the one because he was also the other. He implanted Christianity as extensively and deeply as he did, only because of his profound knowledge of the Mystery of Christ and of God's plan for our salvation. This very knowledge was continually enriched by the experiences of his missionary life.

St. Paul is no theorist. Indeed he was much too sensitive to be able to live in the domain of abstractions. In his *Letters* to the young Christian communities, we shall find this quivering sensitivity, ever on the watch, vibrating to all worries as to all joys. When he expresses his thoughts, Paul also pours out his heart. On each page, his personality stands forth, in all its originality and vigour, in his attachments, in his tenderness, no less than in his anger. A personality to whom nothing can be indifferent.

Paul wrote his *Epistles* in a relatively short space of time, about fifteen years, from 51-52 *(First Letter to the Thessalonians)* to 66–67 A.D. *(Pastoral Epistles)*. During these fifteen years Paul certainly became more experienced, his knowledge of Christ deepened, and his theological thought developed. From the first *Epistles,* Paul already possesses the whole essential of his message, his 'Gospel', as he likes to call it. Besides, don't forget that when he wrote his *First Letter to the Thessalonians,* in 51 or 52, A.D. he had already been converted to Christ for nearly twenty years. He is on his second missionary journey; he has evangelised Cyprus and Asia Minor, he has preached Christ in Athens, he is founding the Corinth community. It is enough to say that from this time, his letters are the fruit of an already long experience of the Christian life, of extensive missionary activity and of incessant meditation on the Mystery of Christ. The *Epistles,* therefore, represent for us the maturity of Paul's thought and the testimony of his whole life. They constitute a block, a whole, marked with a profound unity.

How are we to read these *Epistles* of Paul? As newsreels of the times or as doctrinal expositions? Indeed, they are both one and other. They are the solution to quite practical problems, those which cropped up, as the days flowed along, in the first Christian communities. But Paul treats of these problems and solves them by bringing them back to the essential point, by explaining them by constant reference to the major truths of Chrisianity. In his *Letters,* we never find anything accessory or accidental. Paul goes straight to the heart of the debate, and even his digressions do not deviate from it. As a result, each of his Letters, to all appearances personal and realistic, gives a deeper insight into the only reality which counts for Paul: the Mystery of Christ and of His C hurch. It is useless for us to expect to find anything else in them. No more than any other biblical author does Paul wish to satisfy our curiosity – on the contrary, he only wants to help us to deepen our faith.

We mention deep insight. Indeed, to answer the often scalding and difficult problems, which the life of his churches set him, Paul cannot rest satisfied with reaffirming the elementary data of the Christian faith, nor with merely repeating catechetics – sometimes developed moreover – which he taught. He must discuss, explain, convince. Allright, he accepts the discussion! Better: he himself opens the debate; he analyses, reasons, argues, examines the value of the proofs brought forward; he dialogues with his questioner, even and above all if he is an adversary, and follows him on his own ground. Not that Paul, having done all this, claims to give us an apologetic justification, still less a rational demonstration of the truth of the Christian message. What he wants is to highlight the perfect coherence of God's Design, brought to its full completion in Christ. All his effort at deepening goes 'from faith unto faith', to use his own expression (Rom. 1, 17), and this will always be the most beautiful definition of his work. Under this heading, Paul is, in the New Testament, the typical theologian, as is Ezechiel, author of *Job* and *The Book of Wisdom* (especially ch. 18 and 33), in the Old Testament. Undoubtedly, our Evangelists, especially Saint John, are also theologians: because each one completed a doctrinal work in which the narrative is charged with teaching. But Paul is the theologian in the strictest sense of the term:

the person who by his work of research, of elaboration and of organisation moulds a personal synthesis.

Where did he find the elements of this synthesis? He did not hesitate to borrow them from the very world in which he was living, and with which he could so perfectly identify himself, making himself 'become to the Jews a Jew... to those without the law as one without the Law' (I Cor. 9, 20). He found himself providentially placed, indeed, first of all by his origin, secondly by his conversion, for meeting the Jewish world, the Greek world and the Christian world.

He inherits the whole primitive Christian tradition, and, with it, this first effort at theological elaboration, to which the talks in the beginning of the *Acts* especially bear witness. He thoroughly knows the Old Testament; this is therefore the basis of all discussion and the almost exclusive source of the arguments and proofs. He uses it as a rabbi, formed to the methods of the Jewish teachers of the time, he, Paul who was 'brought up... a pupil of Gamaliel, and instructed' *(Ac. 22, 3)*. However, his manner is always very personal; he is not a servile disciple of academic teaching. He is influenced also by the apocalyptic current, which was, in those times, the continuance of prophetic literature. Hellenism, which he reaches through the Jewish world of the Diaspora (dispersal of Jews), but directly also, provides him with expressions and images and even the formulation of certain problems (such as that of the resurrection of the body, in I Cor. 15).

A very complex whole, obviously. But all these elements are very powerfully unified by one outstanding fact: his own vocation. The vision at Damascus made of Paul the prophet of Christ. Christ 'laid hold' of him, indeed, as God (Jahweh) laid hold of Amos and David *(Phil. 3, 12; Am. 7, 15; II S. 7, 8)*; He consecrated him to His service as Jeremias and the Servant had formerly been consecrated *(Gal. 1, 15; Jer. 1, 5; Is. 49, 1)*; he made of him the universal missionary announced by the Scriptures *(Ac. 13, 47 and 26, 17-18; cf. Is. 49, 6)*. Whoever reads Paul's *Epistles* without keeping constantly before him this vocation, this intervention of Christ in his life will never understand them. At a determined time in his existence, Paul experienced the all-powerfulness of the risen Christ; from that time on, he had no other thought, no other aim, but to know Him more perfectly 'Him and the power of His resurrection' *(Phil. 3, 1)*. To know him and to make him known to all men: for Paul that meant one and the same thing. His missionary labours and his theological work find, in that one thing, their common source. Starting from there Paul's message assumes an ever present prophetic value. It is really a 'Gospel', in so far as this term belongs exactly to the language of prophecy and mission work. Even when he is arguing in the most subtle manner, Paul is neither a dialectician nor a philosopher but a believer and a witness. His work of synthetic theology is not the beautiful construction of a mind endowed with genius. It is, and will ever be, the proclamation of the Good News of our salvation.

This message Paul gives us in very lively language. He wrote his *Letters* in the popular Greek of his time, Koine, but a good Koine. His style is an oral style: Paul used to dictate his *Letters*. Moreover the habit of public speaking had evidently its effect on him, too – he was quite happy to make a speech, to have a turn at oratory. The developments are sometimes heavy and cumbersome (especially in the *Epistles* of the captivity), but they are always absorbing and enticing. Paul is neither a literateur nor a purist; he is a racy writer. Scarcely ever poetic, he is, on the other hand eloquent and dramatic. He is so, spontaneously and naturally. He is so because he writes to convince and because he is very much aware of the greatness of the stakes: the destiny of man himself. Consequently his style is always completely dominated and controlled by his thought. Paul gladly adopts the rhetorical mannerisms of his time: Interrogation, repetition, contrast. But, for him, these are never mere mannerisms: they rise up very naturally from the deep movement of his thought. We cannot suspect him of being a rhetorician, like, for example, Saint Augustine.

His Letters show no affectation, no polish. In these he speaks absolutely freely about all things and all men while being perfectly submissive to God alone and to His Christ. The man, the believer, the Apostle, stands out on every page, in absolute simplicity.

Our century, as each one of the christian centuries which preceded it, perceives this trustworthiness. We recognise ourselves in this man, Paul who gives himself so directly to us. We find in him a brother as well as a model. Therefore each one of us can find the message personally addressed to him or her self.

Brief Reminder of the Life of Saint Paul

One single moment in Paul's life will always be the one of
paramount importance for us: that of the vision of Damascus.

We can situate it accurately enough in the narrative: four
or five years, undoubtedly, after our Lord's death – indeed,
we must suppose a certain development in the Church
already – about the year 34-35 A.D. Paul was then between
25 and 28 years of age.

He was born in the Jewish Diaspora, in Tarsus, in Cilicia,
and belonged to a family deeply attached to the traditions
of his nation. About the age of 16 years, he had come to
Jerusalem to study under the direction of the famous
teacher, Gamaliel, a Pharisee, and member of the Sanhedrin, mentioned in the *Acts of the Apostles (5, 34; 22, 3)*.
In his school, Paul became a sincere Pharisee, a typical
representative of that sect whose religious ideal was in-
contestably high, though tainted with intolerance and
pride. There is, therefore, nothing astonishing in the fact
that we find him again, about ten years later, persecuting
the new-born Church.

It is then he meets, on the Damascus road, the risen
Christ: 'I am Jesus Whom you persecute'. This lightning
vision is for him a new birth... He comes into the Church,
receives Baptism 'and immediately begins to preach Jesus,
in the synagogues of Damascus'.

The years pass: he goes to Arabia, returns to Damascus,
travels to Jerusalem to meet Peter and James there. Then
he returns home again to Tarsus. Barnabas joins him
there in the year 43 A.D. and Paul instantly takes his place
as one of the leading men in the important christian community of Antioch.

This community has a missionary spirit. Paul and Barnabas are soon chosen to go forth and proclaim Christ in
Cyprus and in Asia Minor. This is Paul's first mission; he

17

establishes Christian communities in Pisidia and in Lyconia. The year 48 A.D. after about three years of journeying, he is back in Antioch. He takes part in the Assembly in Jersualem in the year 49 A.D.

That same year, he sets out on another mission, with the intention of visiting his churches and of preaching the Gospel farther away still. He is going to Europe this time. He reaches Greece through Macedonia, also Athens, and stays for a long time in Corinth. This stay gives us one of the best chronological bench-marks for Paul's life. The *Acts* tell us that he appeared before the proconsul Gallio; now an inscription found in Delphi dates the proconsulate of Gallio as 52 A.D. From Corinth, he writes his two *Letters to the Thessalonians*. He returns to Antioch in 52 A.D.

The third mission occurs from 53 A.D. to 57 (or 58) A.D. Paul revisits his communities in Asia Minor and stays for a long time in Ephesus, from where his preaching radiates over the whole Roman province of Asia. He writes in this town the first *Letter to the Corinthians and the Letter to the Galatians,* only that the latter was written a litle later in Corinth. Paul now passes into Macedonia, where he writes his second *Letter to the Corinthians*, then he stays in Corinth. Here he writes his *Letter to the Romans*. From Corinth, he intended to regain Syria directly. But learning that the Jews were weaving a plot against him, he decides to go back through Macedonia. He embarks at Phillippi, from where he reaches Tyre and Cesarea. From there, he proceeds towards Jerusalem, to give to the Mother-Church the proceeds of the collection made in Macedonia and Achaia.

In Jerusalem, in the Temple itself, Asiatic Jews rouse the people to riot against him. Paul would probably have met the same fate that Stephen did before, if the Roman soldiers had not intervened. He was arrested. That marks the beginning of a captivity which was to last for two years in Palestine (58-60 A.D.) and then, because Paul had appealed to Caesar, for a further two years in Rome (61-63) A.D. During his Roman captivity, he writes the *Letters to the Colossians, to Philemon, to the Ephesians,* probably also the *Letter to the Philippians*, although the place of origin and the date of the latter are more discussed.

He was freed in 63 A.D. but imprisoned again in Rome in 67 A.D. We know very little about his last years, except that his *Letters to Titus and Timothy* date from this time. *The Letter to the Hebrews* was written by a disciple of Paul, also in the years 66-67 A.D.

In 67 A.D., Paul suffered martyrdom in Rome.

I

Christ Our Hope

The Two Letters to the Thessalonians

The First Letter to the Thessalonians

During his second missionary journey, when he was in Troas, Paul had a vision. A Macedonian, standing in front of him, addressed this prayer to him. – 'Come over into Macedonia and help us.' Paul set about preparing for Macedonia, certain that God was calling him to spread the Gospel there. Shortly afterwards, he embarked for Neapolis. This was the first time that Paul set foot on European soil. That was in 50-51 A.D. *(Ac. 16, 9)*.

Travelling along the Egnation Road connecting East with West, Paul reached Thessalonica, capital of the Roman province of Macedonia, an important and populous town where the Jews were numerous. In their synagogue, he preached Jesus, the Messiah, crucified and risen. Many Greek proselytes were converted. But the jealousy of the Jews, and soon their declared hostility, obliged Paul to leave the town. He then went to Beroea, then, persecuted again, reached Athens, where he pronounced the celebrated discourse at the Areopagus; at last he reached Corinth *(Ac. 17-18)*.

It is more than likely that Paul wrote his first *Letter to the Thessalonians* at the end of 51 or at the beginning of 52. This young community of Thessalonica was worrying him. He knew that it was in a difficult situation: on one side were the temptations of the pagan world; on the other, the hostility of the Jewish milieu, which was exciting public opinion against the Church... Paul 'being no longer able to bear it' had sent his companion, Timothy *(3, 1)* down there. On the latter's return, he had learned that the Christian group remained faithful and fervent, but that grave matters were disturbing it and risked even dividing it. The young Christians of Thessalonica were anxiously expecting the Day of the Lord; had not Paul announced that Christ would return? When would He return? Would it be soon? There had been a few deaths in the community: what then will be the fate of those Christians who had died before the Return of Christ? Won't they find themselves excluded from His triumph?

Such are the questions to which Paul will reply in this *Letter*. A very simple, very concrete *Letter* which puts us into direct contact with the life of a Pauline Church and reveals to us in a particularly touching manner, what were the relations of the Apostle to his communities. It is neither a polemic writing as are later the *Letter to the Galatians* and *to the Corinthians*, nor a theological exposition like the *Letter to the Romans*. Paul simply tries here to solve the problems of the time, to bring back calm to a somewhat excited community. He does so in an outpouring of affection and of tenderness, even, and with a note of freshness which we may never meet again.

The present Letter has, moreover, a real doctrinal interest. As regards the agenda, we find in this first *Epistle*, the essential themes of Pauline theology.

The tone of this *Letter*, its vocabulary, its style, its doctrine, all is so perfectly typical of Paul that its authenticity is practically undisputed.

A. – *A young Christian Community*

More than any other *Letter* from Paul, this *first Letter to the Thessalonians* gives us an impression of spontaneity, of youth, of fervor. The souvenir that Paul had of his converts in Thessalonica, of their confidence in him, of their welcome for the Gospel, was evidently very vivid. Paul had known, in this new-born community, an atmosphere which he had perhaps never met before and which contrasted greatly with the welcome at Athens, and even at Corinth, from where he writes this letter.

Hence his first gesture is to give thanks to God for this community, for its fidelity, for its courage under trial. Certainly other Letters of Paul will begin, also, by an act of thanksgiving. We know, also that thanks to God for the good health of the addressee, the good news received, etc., belonged to epistolary style then common. But what a difference in tone between these profane letters and those of Paul! What a difference, even between the acts of thanksgiving in *The Letter to the Corinthians* or to the *Philippians* and those in the profane! In Paul's, in spite of the inevitable preoccupations, the dominant note is confidence and affection:

> 'We give thanks to God always for you all, continually making a remembrance of you in our prayers; being mindful before God our Father of your work of faith, and labour, and charity, and your enduring hope in our Lord Jesus Christ.
> We know, brethren, beloved of God, how you were chosen. For our gospel was not delivered to you in word only, but in power also, and in the Holy Spirit and in much fulness, as indeed you know what manner of men we have been among you for your sakes. And you became imitators of us and of the Lord, receiving the word in great tribulation, with joy of the Holy Spirit, so that you became a pattern to all the believers in Macedonia and in Achaia. For from you the word of God has been spread abroad, not only in Macedonia and Achaia, but in every place your faith in God has gone forth, so that we need say nothing further...'   (1, 2-8)

Here, Paul evokes the whole life of youthful Christianity. The community was founded on the Gospel. *The Gospel!* For us, a book... For Paul, the Word of Christ, the proclamation of salvation thanks to Jesus crucified and risen! *The Gospel* is an active reality which transforms the universe: the evangelical Word is creative, because it is the Word of God. It transformed the Thessalonians. It made them 'turn away from idols' (1, 9) to turn towards Christ. Consequently this young Christianity is living, ever since, in the practice of the theological virtues: faith, hope and charity. Timothy, on his return from Thessalonica was able to give Paul good news of this faith and this charity of the Thessalonians (3, 6). But in the discovery of Christ, the

25

converts found something else as well: joy. Not, however, any joy whatever. A joy which bears the seal of its Christian authenticity: joy in the midst of trials. Jesus had revealed it in the 'Beatitudes':

> 'Blessed are they who suffer persecution for justice' sake, for theirs is the kingdom of heaven. Blessed are you when men reproach you, and persecute you, and speaking falsely, say all manner of evil against you, for my sake. Rejoice and exult, because your reward is great in heaven; for so did they persecute the prophets who were before you.' *(Mt. 5, 10-12)*

This joy, the prophets, persecuted indeed for justice' sake, had not discovered: a discouraged and bitter Elias was demanding death *(1Kg. 19)*; a Jeremias was calling the vengeance of God on his persecutors, was trying to steal away from his mission, was going as far as cursing the day of his birth *(Jer. 2, 18-23; 20, 7-8)*. Only the Resurrection of Jesus, coming after His Passion, could make us discover joy in suffering: because it revealed its redemptive character. From this on, the Christian knows that his trials unite him to the passion of Christ. Hence he finds in them a deep and supernatural joy: he has become an imitator of his Master, and he knows that his suffering prepares his resurrection in glory as well as his brothers'. Such, indeed, is the joy that the first Christian community knew:

> 'The Apostles departed from the Sanhedrin, rejoicing that they had been counted worthy to suffer disgrace for the Name of Jesus.' *(Ac. 5,41)*

This is really the 'joy of the Holy Spirit' which the absolute certainty born at Pentecost alone can give. Paul has the right to say to his converts in Thessalonica:

> 'For you, brethren, have become imitators of the churches of God which are in Judea in Christ Jesus, in

that you also have suffered the same things from your own countrymen as they have from the Jews, who both killed the Lord Jesus and the prophets, and have persecuted us... they hinder us from speaking to the gentiles, that they may be saved.' *(2, 14-15)*

This fidelity of such a youthful and so tried a community bears brilliant witness to the power of the Word of God. If this divine efficacy of the Gospel was revealed in the first days in the conversion of the Thessalonians, it stands out, mow more than ever, in the firmness of their faith. Paul is a believer who speaks to believers: he wants to make them grasp what he himself sees, this efficiency of the divine Word the 'Word of God Who works in you who have believed' *(2, 13)*. Later, in his *Letter to the Romans,* a synthetic work which will give definite formulas, Paul will call the Gospel 'the power of God unto salvation to everyone who believes' *(Rom. 1, 16)*. His whole Apostolic career was founded on the supernatural power of the Christian message.

The Christian vocation is a vocation to hope. The Thessalonians understood this well. If they were living in joy, if they remained firm in their faith, it is because they were expecting from the heavens 'the Son of God' Jesus, His Son, Whom He raised from the dead, Who has delivered us from the wrath to come' (1, 10).

It is possible that this very beautiful expression, which is the prelude to our Credo: 'from whence He shall come to judge the living and the dead' has been borrowed by Paul from one of the first symbols of the Christian faith. It has quite a primitive flavour. It evokes not only the discourse at Athens, where Paul announced 'the day on which He will judge the world with Justice by a Man Whom He has appointed, and Whom He has guaranteed to all by raising Him from the dead' *(Ac. 17, 31)*, but, more directly still, Peter's discourse after the cure of the infirm man in the Temple:

(...) Repent therefore and be converted, that your sins may be blotted out in order that, when the times of refreshment shall come from the presence of the Lord He may send Him Who has been preached to you, Jesus Christ. For heaven indeed must receive Him until the times of the restoration of all things... *(Ac. 3, 19-21)*

In another Letter of Paul himself, we find the ancient Aramaic expression Maranatha, Come, Lord *(I Cor. 16, 22)*, having passed from the first Judeo-Christian communities into those of the Greco-Roman world. This ancient formula of hope occurs again in Saint John's *Apocalypse:* 'Come, Lord Jesus' *(Apoc. 22, 17-21)*.

This expectation of the return is essential to the Christian faith. And Paul teaches us, as well as the Thessalonians, that the expected Judge is also, and first of all, a Saviour. He 'Who has delivered us from the wrath to come' is the manifestation of the justice of God on a guilty world. Anger announced by the prophets in their visions of punishment, and by the last of them, John the Baptist, when he was preaching on the banks of the Jordan *(Mt. 3, 7 – Lk. 3, 7)*. Anger which will soon be unleashed against the Jews, as Jesus announced *(Lk. 21, 23)*. Anger that Paul himself, in his *Letter to the Romans* will see 'For the wrath of God is revealed from heaven against all ungodliness and wickedness of men' *(Rom. 1, 18)*. But we, the believers, we know that we are purified from our sins in the blood of Jesus Christ. We know that in the risen Jesus, we have an intercessor always living for us beside the Father. That is why our expectation of the Day is not anxious but joyful and confident. We know that God calls us 'to His Kingdom and to His glory' *(1, 12)*.

B. – *The Heart of Paul*

Paul is himself quite captivated by the souvenirs which he has begun to evoke. He feels also all the good that their recall can do to this young community, and he is going to pause a moment to tell us what has been its attitude to him, the Apostle, at the time of the foundation of the Church in Thessalonica.

> 'For you yourselves, brethren, know that our coming among you was not in vain. But although we had previously experienced suffering and shameful treatment at Philippi, as you know, we had confidence in our God[1] to preach the Gospel of God amid much anxiety.'
>
> *(2, 1-2)*

Such is the first witness that Paul gives us of his apostolic experience. The essential spiritual gift of the Apostle, which he reveals to us here is assurance[1] or 'boldness'. It is difficult to make the exact sense of this word clear, on account of its hidden wealth of meaning. It means a boldness in speech and action, which does not worry about opposition, which does not allow itself be intimidated by threats, or weakened by seductions. A liberty which does not allow itself be hindered by any worldly considerations: honour, success, opinion, scandal. Such is the first quality of the Apostle; and he owes it not to himself, not to his character, not to his intelligence, not to his courage, but to God, to the Holy Spirit. Thus we read in the *Acts* that the Apostles Peter and John, simple men, who before Pentecost would not have dared speak in public, presented themselves before the Sanhedrin with a disconcerting assurance or 'boldness'.

> 'Now seeing the boldness[1] of Peter and John, and finding that they were uneducated and ordinary men, the Sanhedrites began to marvel.' *(Ac. 4, 13)*

Thus, too, the prayer of the Christian community threatened by the Jews is simply this:

> 'And now, Lord, take note of their threats, and grant to Thy servants to speak Thy word with all boldness[1].'
>
> *(Ac. 4, 29)*

Translator's Note: 1. The original French word, in each case, is 'assurance'.

Now if God's envoy, the Apostle, can possess such assurance before men, such liberty, an almost entire boldness, it is definitely because he has in view no earthly interest, but God alone:

> 'For our exhortation was not from error, nor from impure motives, nor from guile. But as approved by God to be entrusted with the Gospel, so we speak not as pleasing men, but God, Who proves our hearts. For at no time have we used words of flattery, as you know, nor have we sought glory from men, neither from you nor from others. Although as the Apostles of Christ we could have claimed a position of honour among you.' (2, 3-7)

Here, Paul undoubtedly aims at other 'Apostles' in the wider sense of the word, preachers who were going from church to church, seeking to draw profit from their word or to impose their personal authority on communities. This is the first time that we meet an allusion to such people; it is not the last. In Galatia, in Corinth, and even during his captivity, Paul will have to fight, sometimes in a very violent way, these so-called apostles, who used to come along criticising his person and his work and trying to impose their personal views, for motives more or less interested.

The real Apostle behaves in a totally different way. Here is the description that Paul gives us of him, one of the most beautiful and moving available:

> 'While in your midst we were as children: as if a nurse were cherishing her own children, so we in our love for you would gladly have imparted to you not only the Gospel of God, but also our own souls; because you had become most dead to us.
>
> For you remember, brethren, our labour and toil. We worked night and day so as not to be a burden to any of you while we preached to you the Gospel of God. You are witnesses and God also, how holy and just and blameless was our conduct towards you who have believed;

inasmuch as you are aware of how we entreated and comforted each one of you, acting towards you as a father towards his children declaring to you that you should walk worthily of God, who called you unto His kingdom and glory.' *(2, 7-12)*

These are no mere expressions of human affection. Don't we find in them the echo of these passages of the Old Testament, where God Himself compares His tenderness, to that of a father; to that of a mother?

'The Lord Thy God has carried thee, as a man is wont to carry his little son, all the way that you have come until you came to this place.' *(Dt. 1, 31)*

'As the eagle, enticing her young to fly, And hovering over them, He spread his wings, and has taken him, And carried him on his shoulders.' *(Dt. 32, 11)*

'And I was like a foster-father to Ephraim, I carried them in my arms. I will draw them with cords. With the bands of love. I will be to them as one who raises a nursling against his cheeks, I bent towards him to give him something to eat.'

(Os. 11, 3-4)

Did not Jesus Himself compare Himself to 'the hen Who gathers her chickens under her wings'.

(Mt. 23, 37) & (Lk. 13, 34)

Such is the genuine context of the witness that Paul gives us. The affection, the tenderness of the Apostle for his young community is quite a different thing from the geniality of a man. t has its source in the love of God for Israel, in the charity of Jesus for His people. Just as Moses was ordered by God to 'Carry them in thy bosom, as the nurse is wont to carry the little infant' *(Num. 11, 12)* the Apostle holds the place of the Lord and must give testimony, first of all, of his infinite charity. Charity has nothing to do with sentiment, but is the gift of oneself: like the Good Shepherd, Paul is ready to give his life for his sheep. He insists also, and will do so very often in other letters that he was not a burden to the community. However, he will write a little later to these same christians of Thessalonica that he perfectly understands his rights in this matter *(II, Th. 3, 9)*; and he will remind them forcibly, in his *Letter to the Corinthians,* of 'the rule established by the Lord: those who preach the Gospel live by the Gospel' *(I Cor. 9, 14)* cf. *(Lk. 10, 7).* But Paul did not want to use this right, and he will never use it. He used to earn his living working with his hands, undoubtedly weaving cloth for tents *(Ac. 18, 3).* Moreover, we know that the rabbis of the time used to practise, voluntarily, manual work of a mechanical type. If the Greco-Roman world despised manual work, servile work, reserved for slaves, the Jewish world, on the contrary, thought highly of it. Paul, having become a Christian missionary, kept this habit, therefore. In it He saw a sure way of not depending on anyone, of being, consequently, entirely free, in all circumstances to express his feelings, his judgements, his reproaches to the communities that he had founded. But there is more to it than that. Paul tells us himself that he 'was as a child' in the midst of his own. He could get himself treated like the chief and the master that he really was *(Jn. 13, 13)*; but he longed to live his life like any one of his Christian brothers, in the simplicity of an ordinary condition, among these poor people, the converts of Thessalonica.

In all Paul's *Letters,* we shall find evidence of his Apostolic heart and soul. None of it, perhaps, is as simple and as moving as that which he gives here.

C. – *The ideal of the Christian*

The world in which the new Christians lived put on hard trial, not only their faith in the one God, but their moral life. Paul used to ask them to 'To lead a life pleasing unto God' *(4, 1)*; but that was almost asking daily heroism from men plunged in the pagan milieu where debauch, in all its forms, was prevalent everywhere, since the gods themselves gave the example of vice! Of course, pagans could reach an elevated moral ideal; but the mass, in which these new Christians lived, were abandoning themselves too often to licentiousness.

Now, from the first minute, the Christian ideal took up its stand against this pagan immorality, in all its firmness, its rigour, even its austerity and its uncompromising intransigence.

> 'For this is the will of God, your sanctification; that you abstain from immorality; that every one of you learn how to possess his vessel in holiness and honour, not in the passion of lust like the Gentiles who do not know God; that no one transgress and over reach his brother in the matter, because the Lord is the avenger of all these things, as we have told you before and have testified. For God has not called us unto uncleanness, but unto holiness. Therefore, he who rejects these things rejects not man but God, who has also given His Holy Spirit to us.' *(4, 3-8)*

These Christian requirements are the same as those of the Law of Sinai. The words of Paul 'For this is the will of God, your sanctification', are, as it were, the echo of *Genesis:* 'Walk before me and be perfect' *(Gen. 17, 1)*. Indeed, Jesus did not abolish the ideal of the Ancient Law. He revised it, refined it, deepened it, as the 'Sermon on the Mount' shows. The Apostles taught this New Law, the Law of Christ (cf. *I Cor. 9, 21*). It was important that the new Christians should become aware of these obligations, but, above all, that they should understand their profound source. Paul, in one word, reveals this clearly to us; it is the presence in us of the Holy Ghost. Just as the presence of God in the midst of His people was for Israel a permanent requirement of sanctity, so also the gift of the Spirit to Christians is for them an incessant call to sanctity. The moral ideal of Christianity, and also of the Old Testament, does not spring from a philosophy, a certain conception of man, an innate sense of duty or from a search for reasonable happiness; it springs from the certainty of a presence 'He has given His Holy Spirit to you'; Paul's phrase insists on this 'to you'. Moral life appears as the blossoming forth in the Christian, of the vocation received just when the Holy Spirit takes possession of him, at baptism.

> 'But concerning brotherly charity there is no need for us to write to you, for you yourselves have learned from God to love one another. For indeed you practise it towards all the brethren all over Macedonia. But we exhort you brethren, to make even greater progress. Strive to live peacefully, minding your own affairs, working with your own hands, as we charged you, so that you may walk becomingly towards outsiders, and may need nothing.'
> (4, 9-12)

Fraternal charity: such is the great commandment of Christianity, as it was already that of the old Law; it says: 'Love thy neighbour as thyself' (Lk. 19, 18). This commandment, so profoundly human, does not come from man. 'You have learned from God Himself, says Paul, to love one another.' Indeed the prophet Isaias had announced that in messianic times all the sons of the chosen people would be 'taught by God' (Is. 54, 13), and Jesus recalls this promise in His 'Discourse on the Bread of Life' (Jn. 6, 45). Without any doubt, it is of this interior teaching that Paul is thinking here; silent teaching of divine grace, teaching of the Spirit in the soul of the believer. Paul speaks to us in another letter, of 'words taught by the Spirit' (I Cor. 2, 13). He knows indeed that we, the chosen ones of God, in these times which are the last times, are living under the interior motion of the Spirit of God.

He adds a few recommendations, apparently very simple, in reality charged with a very precise meaning: Live peacefully, says he, mind your own affairs, work... So there were in the community sowers of troubles and lazy people? Of course! because they were worried about the fate of the dead! Since Paul's departure, a few deaths had taken place in the community. The people were asking one another: these brethren, dead before the return of the Lord, announced by Paul, would they share in His triumph? and How? Certain people were so excited by these matters that they forgot, on account of them, to attend to their affairs in the normal way. Paul will answer them; but first he longed to make them realise that true Christian charity is an enemy to trouble-making which always risks creating divisions, and that it shows itself in the humble daily practice of the duty of one's state in life.

D. – *The dead and the return of Christ*

The community of Thessalonica is, therefore, upset about its dead. Paul cannot leave it in ignorance. Remember that these Christians were quite new converts; to them, Paul had been able to give only a very elementary oral teaching, which had been interrupted suddenly, by the persecution which made him leave the town. Today he is going to complete the instruction which he had no time to develop sufficiently. He understands the grief of his dear Thessalonians. For them the great reality is the return of Christ and His triumph, in which all His own must share. That some might be shut out from it, is for them a great sorrow. Paul wants to give them back the joy of hope.
But, after all, has he to add something to what he has already taught them? Don't they know the essential?

'For if we believe that Jesus died and rose again, so with Him God will bring those also who have fallen asleep through Jesus.'   *(4, 14)*

That is the foundation of all our hope. Jesus died, but he rose; so, those who die in Him will rise like Him. Paul does not need to give any further explanation of his thought to people as faithful as the Thessalonians, to whom his great ideas were already, evidently, familiar. But, on the other hand, we must restore the missing link in his reasoning. This link, is faith in our intimate union with Christ by baptism and the life of grace. We know, from other *Letters* of Paul, that this was one of the major themes of his preaching, always accompanying the essential theme: the proclamation of the risen Jesus.

Now, if we are united to Jesus by baptism, grafted on him so as to form with Him but one body, we understand that this union must find its completion in a resurrection like His own. 'Those who have fallen asleep through Jesus', that is 'Those who die in the Lord' are those who died united to Him by faith and grace. They can never be separated from their chief on the Day of His glorious Coming; How could they be since this will be the triumph of that Resurrection in which, by their baptism, they have begun to participate? That sovereign power which God displayed in the Resurrection He will display again to re-unite them definitely to Himself.

But how can this happen? Paul knows well that his Thessalonians are thirsting for information. Here is what he says to them to appease them:

> 'We who live, who survive until the coming of the Lord, shall not precede those who have fallen asleep. For the Lord Himself with cry of command, with voice of arch-angel, and with trumpet of God will descend from heaven; and the dead in Christ will rise up first. Then we who live, who survive, shall be caught up together with them in the clouds to meet the Lord in the air, and so we shall ever be with the Lord.' (4, 15-17)

Don't seek there a description of the Last Day. Paul did not want to satisfy a curiosity which would be merely human. Neither here, nor in the eschatological development of the Letter to the Corinthians (*I Cor.* 15, 20) does Paul wish to give information about the End of the world. No more than any other biblical author does he ever wish to inform; he wants to teach. He does not intend to enrich our knowledge but he does mean to deepen our faith.

Therefore the descriptive elements: cry of command, voice of archangel, trumpet, are very simple and traditional. Here Paul teaches us nothing new. He only draws from the classic descriptions of the Jewish and Christian apocalypse. The details which he mentions recall notably the 'Eschatological Discourse' of Jesus in *The Gospel according to St. Matthew* and as well the *Apocalypse* of Saint John. But he stresses neither these details nor the unrolling of the events.

What he affirms, as an absolute certainty, is that the Lord will return, 'will descend from heaven', according to his own expression, a very simple and biblical expression. What he longs to make clear, 'in the Word of the Lord', which means supported by the authority of God and of Christ, is that Christians, already dead, will suffer no disadvantage at the time of the Return of the Lord. They will rise at that very moment, in such a way as to as to be carried up with us 'in the air', just like Jesus going up to heaven to receive there the glory of His resurrection.

All this is but the logical working out of Paul's faith. All those who have lived or are now living in union with the Lord will also share in his triumph and in His glory. No member of His mystical body can be separated from Him, the head. The affirmations of Paul apparently descriptive, are, in reality, purely theological. The exact appointed time on which he insists 'we shall be caught up together[1] with them to meet the Lord in the air' is only the expression of the unity of the mystical body. The essential affirmation, which is the only one that is really important, is the last:

'And so We shall ever be with the Lord.'   (4, 17)

Very simple words which explain the whole of his thought. Christian eschatology is not speculation on the End of the world nor mysterious revelation on our fate at the other

Translator's Note: 1. The original French words are 'en même temps'. Literal translation in English is 'at the same time'.

side of the grave. It is hope in our total union, our definite union with the risen Christ.

Paul, therefore answered the Thessalonian Christians... without answering them. They wanted to be informed; he was content to explain to them the essential data of their faith. Nobody on this earth can say any more about it.

E. – *The day of the Lord*

At any rate, couldn't we know when all this will happen? Of course, this question was already worrying the first Christians, so much the more as their hope was more ardent. But listen to what Paul says:

> 'But of the times and seasons, brethren, you have no need that we write to you, for you yourselves know well that the day of the Lord is to come like a thief in the night. For when they shall say, 'Peace and security' even then sudden destruction will come upon them, as birth pangs upon her who is with child; and they will not escape.'
> *(5, 1-3)*

Thus it is not a question of speculating on the date of the Return of Christ. All searching on this point is useless, all claimed revelation would be false. Paul answered his Christians as Jesus Himself did His Apostles:

> 'But of that day and hour no one knows, not even the angels of heaven, but the Father only.'
> *(Mk. 13, 32 – Mt. 24, 36)*

On the very day of His ascension, to His Apostles, who were asking Him: 'Lord, is it now that you are re-establishing the Kingdom in favour of Israel?' Jesus had replied:

> 'It is not for you to know the times and dates which the Father has fixed by His own authority.' *(Ac. 1, 7)*

The times and the ages Paul used the very expression of Jesus. It is, indeed, a classic expression which belongs to the apocalyptic language of the Jews. Thus we read in the Old Testament that Wisdom, an attribute of God, alone knows 'the events of times and ages' *(Wisdom 8, 8)* and that God is He 'who changeth times and ages' *(Dan. 2, 21)*. But there again it is not a question of dates and times. It is a question of the sovereign mastery of God over entire history. He alone knows its events, He alone directs them: that is what the biblical texts want to teach us. God mysteriously conducts the destiny of nations and empires towards this Day, which is the Time par excellence, the Last Time. Each one of these epochs, each one of the dates in history is marked by divine intervention, which is the preparation for the great eschatological intervention. No, we do not need to know 'times and ages'; it is enough for us to know by faith that they are all in the hand of God *(cf. Ac. 17, 26)*. Moreover, we need not be afraid of being surprised:

'But you, brethren, are not in darkness, that that day should overtake you as a thief; for you are all children of the light and children of the day, We are not of night, nor of darkness Therefore, let us not sleep as do the rest, but let us be wakeful and sober. For they who sleep, sleep at night, and they who are drunk are drunk at night. But let us who are of the day be sober. Let us put on the breastplate of faith and charity, and for a helmet the hope of salvation. For God has not destined us unto wrath, but to gain salvation through our Lord Jesus Christ, Who died for us in order that, whether we wake or sleep, we should live together with Him.

(5, 4-10)

We are children of the light and children of the day; yes, we are so by our baptism, through which God 'has rescued us from the power of darkness and transferred us into the kingdom of His beloved Son' *(Col. 1, 13)*. From the earliest times of Christianity, baptism has been called 'enlightenment' *(cf. Heb. 6, 4; 10, 32).* The apostle Peter alludes to it without any doubt, when he speaks to us about Him Who 'has called you out of darkness into His marvellous light' *(I Pet. 2, 9),* and the cure of the man born blind, in the *Gospel according to Saint John,* must be understood as a symbol of baptismal enlightenment. The light which we receive thus, is none other than the light of the Resurrection morning, the light of the Day of salvation following the night of death and sin. A primitive christian hymn, which Paul quotes in his *Letter to the Ephesians,* runs:

'Awake, sleeper
And arise from among the dead,
And Christ will enlighten thee.'   *(Eph. 5, 14)*

Let us live then as children of light. Let us watch, that is, let us be always expecting, always ready for the Coming of the Lord, like the faithful servant of whom the Gospel speaks to us *(Mk. 13, 33-37).* Let us be sober, we who are the athletes and soldiers of Christ *(cf. I Cor. 9, 25).* One single reality dominates our whole existence, and gives its sense to our life as well as to our death: our union with Christ, who by His death became for us a source of eternal life.

The Second Letter to the Thessalonians

Several months have passed since Paul's *First Letter*. The community of Thessalonica is showing renewed signs of nervousness and agitation. The difficulties that the *First Letter* revealed to us have cropped up again and increased. The continuing persecution over-excites the people's minds: they hawk round false news, claimed revelations which present *the Day of the Lord* as imminent. One of the most troublesome consequences: certain Christians do not want to work any longer; work is no longer worth the trouble, because the Day is near... They live as parasites and sow dissension in the community.

Reaction is urgent. No, the Day of the Lord has not yet come. Antechrist must appear first; this has not yet happened. Therefore let each one return quietly to his occupations and seek only to do the will of God in the present time. And if anyone does not want to obey let the community react severely with regard to him, in order to make him understand his wrongdoing.

All this, Paul says calmly and kindly but with a firmness of tone not in the first *Letter*. It is understandable that he was annoyed enough, and undoubtedly judged his church of Thessalonica less favourably than in the beginning.

This Second Letter to the Thessalonians asks some critical questions. Some expositors of Scripture thought that they observed differences of style and some contradictions between this Epistle and the preceding; and, moreover, resemblances which are almost repetitions. Certain people wanted to conclude from this fact that this *Second Letter* might be the work, not of Saint Paul himself, but of a clever imitator.

In reality, resemblances just like differences can be easily explained: the problems are practically the same, but the situation has evolved. This is no argument against the Pauline authenticity of this *Epistle*.

It was written, very probably, in the year 52, at Corinth, where Paul was still staying with Silas and Timothy.

A. – Sufferings and kingdom

The First Letter of Paul did not appease the Christians of Thessalonica, far from it. In this year 52, excitement reigned in the community. Its worry about the day of the Lord got worse, its questions more anxious than ever. It is absolutely indispensable that Paul should intervene with all his Apostle's authority, and fix things up. A severe and ungrateful task, for the person who is the founder and the father of this young Christianity. Therefore, he wants first of all, to comfort and encourage. If it is troubled, anxious, devoured by feverish expectations of the Lord, it has indeed some reason for being so: it is the victim of the hostility, even the persecution, of those who surround it. That is its excuse; and because these new Christians bear their trials without wavering in their faith, he compliments them. Paul is anxious to stress in the beginning of his letter this beautiful side of community life.

'We are bound to give thanks to God always for you, brethren. It is fitting that we should because your faith grows exceedingly and your charity each one for the others increases. And because of this we ourselves boast of you in the churches of God for your patience and faith in all your persecutions and the tribulations that you are enduring. In this there is a proof of the just judgement of God counting you worthy of the kingdom of God, for which also you suffer.'   *(II, Th. 1, 3-5)*

A trial accepted with faith is equivalent to a sign. Did not Jesus Himself say that 'it was necessary to suffer these things to enter into his glory' *(Lk. 24, 26).* As one who belongs to him, one of His retinue, Paul repeated to his converts: 'it is through many tribulations that we must enter the Kingdom of God' *(Ac. 14, 22).* Moreover, he had already said the same thing to the Christians of Thessalonica in his preceding *Letter (I Th. 3, 4)*. Later, towards the end of his life, he will write to the Philippians:

'I want to hear about you that you are steadfast... Do not be terrified in any way by the adversaries; for this is to them a reason for destruction but to you for salvation.'
(Phil. 1, 27-28)

That is the lesson of the 'Beatitudes' all over again. The true believer accepts suffering courageously, knowing that it prepares him for the kingdom, and leaving it to God's justice to invervene at what God considers the proper time 'to repay with affliction those who afflict you, and to give you who are afflicted rest' *(II Th. 1, 6-7)*. God reserves all vengeance for Himself *(Rom. 12, 19)*. The trial which his faithful undergo is a call to His Justice, which one day will shine forth in all its splendour *(Lk. 18, 7-8)*.

B. – *The coming of the Lord*

Yes, the Lord will return. He will display all His glory, both in the judgement of his adversaries, pagans as well as Jews, and in the salvation of his faithful. In his preaching, Paul had certainly insisted on this hope of the Return. But the young community of Thessalonica is abnormally excited about this subject. So-called inspired people, proclaim that the day of the Lord is absolutely imminent. They circulate a forged letter in which Paul states the same thing. It is high time that the Apostle himself should calm these agitated minds:

'Let no one deceive you in any way, for the day of the Lord will not come unless the apostasy comes first, and the man of sin is revealed, the son of perdition, who opposes and is exalted above all that is called God, or that is worshipped, so that he sits in the Temple of God and gives himself out as if he were God. Do you not

43

remember that when I was still with you, I used to tell you these things? And now you know what restrains him, that he may be revealed in his proper time. For the mystery of iniquity is already at work; provided only that he who is at present restraining it, does still restrain, until he is gotten out of the way.

And then the wicked one will be revealed, whom the Lord Jesus will slay with the breath of His mouth and will destroy with the brightness of his coming.'

(2, 3-8)

Paul tells us that he is only recalling, by making it more precise probably, the teaching that he already gave orally to the Thessalonians. This teaching constitutes a real little Apocalypse, just like the one we already have in the *First Letter To the Corinthians (15, 22-28)* and in the 'eschatological Discourse' of the *Gospels.* The great Apocalypse of Saint John will only develop the same theme.

It is a very mysterious page, but one which it is our duty to try to understand. The determining phrase, around which everything gravitates, is that of apostacy, of the revelation of the adversary. Now apostacy calls up certain words of Jesus Himself in the *Gospel:*

'When the Son of Man comes, will he find, do you think faith on the earth?'   *(Lk. 18, 8)*

'And because iniquity will abound, the charity of the many will grow cold.'   *(Mt. 24, 12)*

And Jesus put them on their guard against the seductions and the temptations that they would meet; a warning that His Apostles, Peter and John especially, often repeated after Him, in their *Letters* to the christian communities. When saying goodbye to the heads of the Church of Ephesus, Paul said to them:

'I know that after my departure fierce wolves will get in among you and will not spare the flock. And from among your own selves men will rise speaking perverse things, to draw away the disciples after them.'

(Ac. 20, 29-30)

So the Last time will be marked by great trials for the faith. From this must we draw the conclusion of mass apostasy? Let us understand, rather, that the Church must always know trial, and the faithful, temptation; that both the one and the other will be particularly hard in the Times immediately preceding the Coming of the Lord in glory. Paul, and also Jesus, wanted, not so much to predict a precise event as to give us a warning.

But, listen, Paul talks to us at the same time about the manifestation of the man of sin, the son of perdition, the adversary. Three terms which mean evidently, one and the same person. His description calls to mind what the *Book of Daniel* said, in a puzzling form, about King Antiochus Epiphane, persecutor of the Jewish religion *(Dan. 11, 36-37. cf. Ez. 28, 2).* Jesus, in His discourse on the end of time alludes to it, and the *Apocalypse* of Saint John speaks to us in mysterious terms. We ought to compare this passage with that of the Beast who gets himself adored *(Apoc. 13, 4).*

It is a matter, therefore of a being who will exercise an unbelievable fascination, so much so as to get himself adored like a God. This person is the one we call Antichrist. It is, without any doubt, according to the text, a human being, an individual, who can be, besides, the head or the representative of a collective movement. Behind him we can guess the presence and the action of Satan, the Adversary par excellence, who will use him to lead the last fight of all.

But this Antichrist cannot show himself for the moment. Someone or something is preventing him from doing so; the Thessalonians know what it is, because Paul told it to them formerly. Hence he does not repeat himself.

Therefore, what can be this obstacle, which restrains Antichrist from showing himself? One might think of the action of the preachers of the *Gospel,* of the radiance of the

Church itself. But how will Paul face 'gotten out of the way'? It implies rather a determined circumstance than a state of things which restrains the manifestation of Antichrist 'for the moment'. The Fathers of the Church in their commentaries on this mysterious text, have suggested: the Roman Empire. Their idea seems much the best. The Roman Empire was a reality which, obviously, imposed itself on Paul's thought as on that of his Christians. If we understand that every apocalypse is a vision of history we shall understand that Paul has made the Roman Empire play a part in his eschatological picture. He does not name it clearly; but Saint John, who makes certain allusions to Rome in his Apocalypse, avoids naming it also. Discretion imposed by prudence, undoubtedly; but also, the habitual tendency of the apocalyptic authors to express themselves preferably in mysterious language.

That Paul might have seen in the Roman order an obstacle to the manifestation of Antichrist, is perfectly within the biblical tradition. For centuries especially since the Great Exile, which had made Israel reflect on the meaning of history, biblical theology affirmed that God holds in His hand the fate of empires and uses them to work out His Design. Their establishment as well as their fall contribute mysteriously to the coming of the Kingdom of God. Successively, Isaiah (chapter, 40-45), Aggeus and Zachary, Daniel had thus justified theologically the Babylonian Empire, the Persian Empire, the Greek Empire. Nothing is more normal than that Paul should have integrated the Roman Empire with his eschatological vision. Even so, he does not wax political; or rather his policy is the policy of faith, and this, too, was always the policy of the Prophets. But how can the Roman Empire restrain Antichrist? Very probably, on account of the order and the peace which it imposes on the world. Already, six centuries earlier, in 520 B.C., the prophet Zacharias was worried about the calm which the Persian Empire made reign in the world:

'They answered the Angel of the Lord and said 'We have walked through the earth, and behold all the earth is

46

inhabited and is at rest'. Then the Angel of God answered and said 'O, Lord of Hosts how long wilt Thou not have mercy on Jerusalem and the cities of Juda, with which Thou hast been angry?' This is now the seventieth year.' *(Za. 1, 11-12)*

If Zachary becomes sad at this universal tranquillity, it is because he knows very well that a general upheaval is to announce the Coming of the Last Times. The Prophet Aggeus has proclaimed, a few weeks earlier:

'Thus saith the Lord of Hosts 'Yet one little while and I will move the heavens, the earth, the sea and the dry land. And I will move all nations, and the desired of all nations shall come; and I will fill this house with glory;' saith the Lord of Hosts.' *(Ag. 2, 6-7)*

In another oracle Aggeus insists still:

'I will move both heaven and earth. I will overthrow the throne of kingdoms, and will destroy the strength of the kingdom of the Gentiles. I will overthrow the chariot and him that rides therein, and the horses and their riders shall come down...' *(Ag. 2, 21-22)*

Besides, have not all the Prophets connected the Coming of the Reign of God with a great cosmic and political upheaval? Jesus Himself resumed this theme in His 'Discourse on the End of Time'. There would have been nothing astonishing in the fact that Paul saw in Roman peace an obstacle to the manifestation of Antichrist. whose appearance will herald the imminence of the Day of the Lord. Paul and his Christians re-read and meditated upon the prophecies; you need not doubt that they were seeking there the 'signs of the times' of which Jesus spoke *(Mt. 16, 3)*.

In his preceding *Letter,* Paul said that the day would come 'like a thief'. This time he indicates its signs. However, it concerns very general signs. Nor does he at all determine its date. These two ideas, suddenness and signs, are both biblical. What Paul has at heart is to make his Thessalonians understand that real hope is not feverish excitement. Live in hope, but keep calm while you are waiting; such is the essential teaching of this passage.

C. – *The daily duty of one's state*

'And we charge you brethren, in the name of our Lord Jesus Christ, to withdraw yourselves from every brother who lives irregularly. (...) For we were not unruly while with you, neither did we eat any man's bread at his cost but we worked night and day in labour and toil, so that we might not burden any of you. Not that we did not have the right to do so, but that we might make ourselves an example for you to imitate us. For indeed when we were with you we used to charge you: if any man will not work, neither let him eat!'

(3, 6-10)

Hope must be well understood: it is not escape from the present world. Paul concludes his eschatological teaching by a return to the reality of daily life. The Christian who would want to forget this reality, in the name of expecting the Lord, would be labouring under an illusion. For the Lord Himself expects each one of us to find Him in the accomplishment of his or her daily duty.

The first aspect of this duty is work. Greco-Roman Society looked down upon manual work which it left to slaves and menials. The Jewish world, however, especially pharisaic milieux, was happy to reconcile the study of Law with a worker's trade. In this way Paul had learned to weave cloth for tents; besides, this work was the speciality of Tarsus, his native town *(Ac. 18, 3)*. During the whole of his life he will ply this trade. He will always be proud of the fact that he is a burden to no church; proud, too, to give an example, which, no matter how simple it is, is not useless. Years later he will show to the ancients of the

Church of Ephesus, his workman's hands, roughened by hard labour:

'You yourselves know that these hands of mine have provided for my needs and those of my companions.'

(Ac. 20, 34)

Paul shows an astoundingly modern sense of the nobility of work and of the dignity of the worker. A new title, added to so many others, which makes of him the model of the apostles of our time.

2

Christ Our Wisdom

The First Letter to the Corinthians

Paul founded the Church of Corinth, during his second missionary journey, in the year 50. From his *Letters to the Thessalonians* we saw that the Apostle, having set out from Antioch to visit the Churches founded by him in Asia Minor, had passed into Europe as a result of the vision of Troas. After having travelled through Macedonia and stayed in Athens, he arrived in Corinth, where he remained for more than eighteen months.

In this town, then one of the most important in the Mediterranean Basin, Paul founded a populous and very lively Christian community, which was going to be one of his glories but also one of his greatest worries. It is precisely for this last reason that it earned for us, two *Epistles* of exceptional richness, in which Saint Paul reveals at once the main ideas of his theology and the dominant characteristics of his human and spiritual personality.

The Letter which we call *First to the Corinthians* was written in this Church during Paul's third missionary journey. At this time Paul was staying in Ephesus, capital of the Asiatic province, a town whose influence was of great use for his apostolic intentions. He was evidently preoccupied about his Churches in Greece, which he will visit at the end of this journey.

From Ephesus, for a start, he writes his *First Letter to the Corinthians*. This Letter is now lost, but a very clear allusion informs us of its existence *(I Cor. 5, 9)*. Now, he receives very disquieting news from the community: they are fighting and divided in the heart of the Church of Corinth. Paul sends Timothy down there, to get exact information for him and to re-establish peace and order, if possible. But while Timothy is on the way, a group of Christians from Corinth arrives in Ephesus. They bring better news; Paul says he is satisfied *(16, 18)*.

In reality, he knows that the problems remain... Moreover,

the community submitted to him various questions concerning marriage, virginity, Christian morality, etc. Paul seizes this opportunity to write again, to tell the community how he judges it, and to remind it what requirements of charity, of humility, of renunciation the message of the Cross implies.

This Letter was written about the end of the year 55. Its authenticity is never doubted now by anyone. The style and language in it are, generally speaking, more elaborate then in the other *Letters,* but the Pauline character of the whole remains undisputed.

It has sometimes been suggested that this *Letter* might be a mixture of several letters written by Paul in various circumstances. But the collisions in the composition are sufficiently explained by the number and variety of the subjects treated. We have no valid reason for doubting the unity of this writing.

A. – *The two wisdoms*

Corinth was one of the most cosmopolitan towns in the Roman world. All social milieux, all currents of thought, all philosophies, all religions met in this great port, open both to East and West. The Christian community founded by Paul must have been very composite. Life was not always easy there, understanding was far from being perfect. Add to this, the taste for theological quarrels, and a certain amount of intellectual pretensiousness; these annoyed Paul so much that he often waxed ironical; we can understand that every kind of difficulty could arise in such an environment.

Indeed, this did not take long to happen. They got a passion for religious discussions; they were divided by diverse obediences, each claiming for itself its great man:

'For I have been informed about you, brethren, by those of the house of Chloe, that there are strifes among you. Now this is what I mean: each of you says, I am of

Paul, or I am of Cephas, or I am of Apollos, or I am of Christ.'   *(1, 11-12)*

Thus in the Church of Corinth, some wanted to attach themselves to Paul: undoubtedly those he had converted himself during his stay. Others had been seduced by the brilliant eloquence of Apollos, who flattered their intellectual pretentions; they used to say to one another that they were 'of him'. Still more claimed to belong to Peter the chief of the twelve, the companion of the Lord; whether Peter (Cephas) himself had had the opportunity of passing through Corinth, or whether, more likely, a group of Judeo-christians had led a campaign of propaganda for him. Finally, some proclaimed themselves, quite simply, of Christ! Undoubtedly, these were a group of gnostics, of troublesome enough mystics who wanted to recognise no other authority but that of Christ the Lord Himself.
Such was the rather desolate picture that the people of Chloe painted for Paul of the situation in their community. Paul has but one means of getting out of this fix. It is neither discussion nor the comparison of one set with the other, it is an immediate return to Christ Who unites all:

'Has Christ been divided up? Was Paul crucified for you? Or were you baptised in the name of Paul?' *(1, 13)*

Into this Roman world, so deeply divided into Jews and Greeks, free men and slaves, *(Gal. 3, 28)* Paul wanted to bring unity, because he had discovered Christ. 'All men are but one in Christ', there is Paul's message *(Gal. 3, 27)*. He will be so much aware of this that he will write later to the Philippians, when speaking about preachers who did not wish him well:

'But what of it? Provided only that in every way, whether in pretence or in truth, Christ is being proclaimed; in this I rejoice, yes and I shall rejoice.'
                                                          (Phil. 1, 18)

Therefore how abnormal for Christians to be divided! By their baptism they and Christ have become one; how can they be separated, how can they oppose one another? Let them return therefore, to the essential point; far above party cliques and spiritual families, stand the Gospel, and the Cross of Christ.

Yes, the whole Gospel is resumed in the Cross, and this the Corinthians have not yet fully understood. Too easily believing themselves heirs of the great Greek tradition of philosophy and of eloquence, they are inclined to seek in Christianity a new philosophy, which will satisfy their pretensions to 'wisdom'... Wisdom! a magic word which evoked all Greek culture and its most illustrious representatives, back as far as the Ionian Sages of the sixth century. When Paul, after the vision of Troas, had crossed the Aegean Sea to land in Macedonia, Christianity met a new world. In truth, it was not yet visible in Philippi, Thessalonica, or Beroea. But, in Athens and Corinth, there were evidences of christianity. Of course, Greek culture had spread throughout the whole Meditteranean Basin, and all the big towns of the Orient, with Alexandria at their head, belonged really to the Hellenistic world. But, this Hellenistic world was not Greece; and Christianity, for its part, remained all the time, near its Palestinian origins. In Athens, in Corinth, the data of the problem were changing. Paul had noticed this at the time of his stay in the Capital:

'Some of the Epicurean and Stoic philosophers debated with him; and some said 'What is this babbler trying to say?' But others, 'He seems to be a herald of strange gods, because he proclaimed to them Jesus and the Resurrection.' And they took him and brought him to the Areopagus, saying, 'may we know just what is this new doctrine which thou teachest? For thou bringest some strange things to our ears; we wish therefore to know what these things mean'.'   (Ac. 17, 18-20)

Paul did not fail to answer this invitation. He was too conscious of his duty to every one, Greeks and Barbarians, too conscious of his personal vocation, as Apostle to the Hellenistic world, to let this opportunity of preaching and proclaiming Jesus pass. But he had understood that this audience was very different from that of Damascus or Antioch.

He made an address to this audience of philosophers in the language which the Jewish apologetics of the time always used when addressing the pagan world, and which he himself had already had several opportunities of using:

'God Who made the world and all that is in it, since He is Lord of heaven and earth, does not dwell in temples built by hands; neither is He served by human hands as though He were in need of anything, since it is He who gives to all men life and breath and all things.'

(*Ac. 17, 24-25; cf. 14, 15-17*)

Until then they had listened politely to him; but when he had proclaimed:

'God has fixed a day on which He will judge the world with justice by a man whom He has appointed, and whom He has guaranteed to all by raising Him from the dead.' (*Ac. 17, 31*)

his audience had abandoned him; some mocking him and others saying: 'We will hear thee again on this matter' (*Ac. 17, 32*).

In spite of the conversion of Denys, one of the members of the Areopagus, and of some other Athenians, Paul had carried away a disappointing impression of this town. These philosophers as they called themselves, were decidedly too conceited, too sure of themselves and their wisdom, to open up to the preaching of Christ. Further more, wasn't there a radical contradiction, a definite incompatibility between this human wisdom and the message of the Cross? Useless trying to make them agree? Didn't the result prove his own error to the man Paul, himself? These artifices in language, this subtlety of thought, to which he had thought he ought to have recourse, wasn't it all pure nonsense?

Better to give it up. If Corinth was no less eager than Athens for beautiful thoughts and beautiful language, Paul refused to satisfy it.

He did refuse, in fact. And the Corinth milieu less formalistic and more mixed than that of Athens, had shown itself more receptive for his message. But these Corinthians remained Greeks. Their town contained a number of schools and gymnasiums. Even the less wealthy people, of whom the Christian community were mainly composed, were more or less marked by this general atmosphere of culture and of civilisation. In spite of themselves, they turned towards this wisdom composed of human values only: intelligence, wit, words, artistic and technical success. Their judgements of value were not Christian.

Therefore, energetically and severely, Paul will remind them in his preaching:

> 'Christ sent me to preach the Gospel, not with wisdom of words lest the Cross of Christ be made void. For the doctrine of the Cross is foolishness to those who perish, but to those who are saved, that is, to us it is the power of God (...) For the Jews ask for signs and the Greeks look for 'wisdom'; but we for our part, preach a crucified Christ – to the Jews indeed a stumbling block and to the Gentiles foolishness, but to those who are called, both Jews and Greeks, Christ, the power of God and the wisdom of God.' *(1, 17-24)*

Now we see it all in a flash; in the world two wisdoms fight in opposing camps. One, that which Saint John would have called the 'wisdom of the world': that of the Greeks, an ideal of culture and civilisation which makes man the measure of everything, which places him in the centre of the universe not as its head – this the Bible does – but as its god, and nothing is more contrary to our faith. A way of judging of everything with reference to man, of appreciating everything with reference to man, of appreciating everything according to 'flesh and blood' as the Scripture would say, only according to the norms of human thought and human action[1].

No matter how paradoxical it may appear, we must join this wisdom of the Greeks to that of the Jews. Paul did not forget that there were Christians, converted from Judaism in the Corinth community. Over and above them, this minority who had answered grace, his thought embraced all those Jews whom he saw shutting themselves off from the Gospel message. In all the towns through which he passed, he addressed them first. People listened to him as long as he recalled the promises made to Abraham and as long as he evoked the glorious future proclaimed by the prophets. But when he got as far as Jesus, His passion and Cross, he met with total misunderstanding, violent refusal and soon systematic persecution. How strangely parallel was the attitude of the Greeks and that of the Jews! As different as were these peoples, their reactions were the same when faced with the Cross!

These Jews, also, have their human wisdom. They do not, however, place it in the intellectual, artistic or technical conquests of man. On the contrary, they affirm that the only wisdom lies in the Word of God, in His revelation, in His Law. Nevertheless, this divine Word they interpret in a human manner, according 'to flesh and blood', as Jesus already reproached them with:

> 'For letting go the commandment of God, you hold fast
> the tradition of men.' *(Mk. 7, 8)*

Thus the Jews carry out a real perversion of the wisdom of God revealed to them. Is it hope in a Messiah that is under discussion? They only want to retain the promises of glory made to their people. Hence, their minds are no longer

Author's Note: 1. Compare with the words of Jesus to Peter: 'Blessed art thou, because flesh and blood have not revealed this to thee!'

open to the things of Christ. They made for themselves a Christ to the image of their own dreams, a Christ who multiplies miracles, and makes Israel triumphant in the midst of the nations. Today, in their discussions with Paul, as yesterday with Jesus, the Jews ask for signs.

'Master, we would see a sign from Thee (...) 'An evil and adulterous generation demands a sign and no sign shall be given it, but the sign of Jonas the prophet'.'

(Mt. 12, 38-39)

But that sign the Jews will not understand, because to understand the Resurrection they must have accepted the Cross.

The Cross! Neither Greeks nor Jews can accept it. Their wisdom is opposed to it. By refusing to accept the Cross their wisdom shows itself a complete failure. True wisdom, a wisdom worthy of this name, would understand that God can very well display all His power in the weakest 'vessels', in a manner directly contrary to the human manner of judgement. Better still, a truer wisdom would realise that such vessels and such manners of action are the most worthy of God! Does not God wish that we should hold everything from Him, and from Him alone? Is it not greater and more worthy of Him and of His glory to act through the weakest vessels and means, provided that His power shines forth more clearly as a result. Such is the real revelation of the Old Testament, from the vocation of Abraham to the triumph of the Servant of God. Such is the teaching of Jesus, inaccessible to 'the intelligence of man' *(Mt. 16, 23)*. Such is the Christian message, that Paul resumes admirably here, before taking it up again and developing it, a little later, in his *Letter to the Romans:*

'But the foolish things of the world has God chosen to put to shame the 'wise', and the weak things of the world has God chosen to put to shame the strong, and the base things of the world and the despised has God chosen, and the things that are not, to bring to naught the things

that are; lest any flesh should pride itself before Him
(...) so that, just as it is written, 'Let him who takes
pride, take pride in the Lord'.'[1]   *(I Cor. 1, 27–28)*

B. – *Wisdom and charity*

Man must, therefore, enter into the Mystery of the Wisdom
of God. Can he do so of his own accord? Obviously, no.
Only the grace of God gives access to it, only the Spirit of
God can open our intelligences to these superior realities:

'For who among men knows the things of a man save
the spirit of the man which is in him? Even so, the
things of God no one knows but the Spirit of God.'

(I Cor. 2, 11)

He alone, who is really in communion with the Spirit of
God, enters into the divine mysteries. All Christians have
received the Spirit in their baptism, in their confirmation.
But all do not let themselves be led by the Spirit. There is
no denying it, many forget His presence and do not bother
about this supernatural influence which should penetrate
their whole life. The Corinthians, the greater part of them
at any rate, were already Christians, believers certainly,
and very attached to their faith, but easily forgetful of the
divine presence of the Spirit within them. Paul reproaches
them, in a tone at once severe and paternal, the tone which
he always uses towards this community, more turbulent
than wicked:

'And I, Brethren, could not speak to you as to spiritual
men but only as carnal, as to little ones in Christ. I fed
you with milk, not with solid food, for you were not yet

Author's Note: 1. This text recalls the words of Jesus: 'I praise
Thee, Father, Lord of heaven and earth, that Thou didst hide
these things from the wise and prudent, and didst reveal them
to little ones.'

(Mt. 11, 25)

61

ready for it. Nor are you now ready for it, for you are still carnal. For since there are jealousy and strife among you, are you not carnal and walking as mere men?'   *(3, 1-3)*

Paul gives us the decisive criterion: where charity is missing, the Spirit of God does not really reign. Jealousies divisions, oppositions are also contrary to Him who is the Spirit of unity. Those who take part in them are not, on that account, cut off from the Church, but they show that they do not live their baptism fully. They still yield to vanity, egoism, party-spirit, to the desire of making their ideas triumph and of passing them off for the faith itself. All this does not come from God but from man. All this is 'carnal,' which does not mean sensual but earthly: the Purely instinctive reaction of man who forgets his new birth.

Christians who present the painful spectacle of division, like the Corinthians, are not, therefore, adult Christians; they are not yet fully aware of the responsibilities of their baptismal engagement. They are yet but 'little children in Christ'. So they must be treated, and Paul regrets having to do this.

On the contrary, all those who let themselves be led by the Spirit of God, who live fully as sons of God are really spiritual men, 'Mature' to use another word of Paul *(2, 6)*. They are the really wise Christians. Because Christian wisdom does not consist, as the Corinthians were too inclined to believe, in brilliant theories, but in a life wholly penetrated with divine love: love of God, love of his brothers.

The Apostle does not speak to them as to little children, but as to adults in Christ. He can give them, as he says in the *Letter to the Hebrews:* 'solid food which is for the mature, for those who by practice have their faculties trained to discern good and evil' *(Heb. 5, 14)*.

So, what is this 'solid food'? Paul tells us himself: 'the wisdom of God, mysterious, hidden, which God foreordained before the world unto our glory' *(2, 7)*. It is again 'what (things) God has prepared for those who love Him' *(2, 9)*; or 'the things that have been given us by God' *(2, 12)*. Finally it is 'the deep things of God' *(2, 10)*. All expressions which evoke a profound teaching of the Design of God for our salvation, such as, for example, Paul will sketch in the *Letter to the Romans (8, 18-30)*, and, later still, in the *Letter to the Ephesians*; where he will write:

> 'That the God of our Lord Jesus Christ, the Father of glory, may grant you the spirit of wisdom and revelation in deep knowledge of Him: the eyes of your mind being enlightened, so that you may know what is the hope of His calling, what the riches of the glory of his inheritance in the saints, and what the exceeding greatness of his power towards us who believe.'   *(Eph. 1, 17-19*

Like all really spiritual people, Paul used to love to ponder upon these heavenly realities in which we begin to share here below; full possession of them is reserved for the world 'of the saints' where we shall share the glory of the angels, even the glory of God Himself. There, in perfect communion with Christ and His Father we shall contemplate the depths of God, that is, the infinite richness of His grace, of which we have only a faint notion while we are still living here below:

> 'We see now through a mirror in an obscure manner, but then face to face. Now I know in part, but then I shall know even as I have been known.'   *(13, 12)*

Really spiritual Christians are orientated towards these eschatological realities. Let us understand thoroughly that, for them, it is not at all a matter of searching for speculative knowledge. They must get to understand daily more and more what it is 'to be risen with Christ, seated in heaven with Him,' and conform their lives to this. In this fulness of knowledge and of charity, the transforming action of the Holy Ghost is revealed.

C. – *Christian requirements*

Paul knew what he was talking about when he reproached the Christians of Corinth with being 'carnal' and with behaving in a merely human way. Their community not only presented the spectacle of divisions and party oppositions. There was among them a Christian whose conduct was a public scandal, and the community did not react! It was to be wondered if the people thought that conduct almost normal, in any case tolerable.

Paul, therefore, had to intervene. He does so with energetic indignation. He condemns the guilty man, he excommunicates him from the Christian assembly, hoping however, that God will pardon him and save him. But the whole community merits a severe reprimand for its passivity. How did it happen that the community did not understand that such a scandal was for it a shame and a danger?

> 'Do you not know that a little leaven ferments the whole lump? Purge out the old leaven, that you may be a new dough as you really are without leaven. For Christ, our passover, has been sacrificed. Therefore let us keep festival, not with the old leaven, nor with the leaven of malice and wickedness but with the unleavened bread of sincerity and truth.' *(5, 6-8; Mt. 16, 6-11)*

This shows that what the Corinthians did not understand was the very foundation of Christian morality itself. Christians, from the moment of Baptism, have entered into their Last Passover. Their life is an incessant liturgy, as Ezechiel announced when he described the new Israel. The unique and eternal sacrifice of this liturgy, is that of Christ; He sacrificed Himself, becoming thus our Paschal Lamb, of which that of the Jewish Pasch was but the figure.

Therefore we must celebrate the feast of unleavened bread (azymes), which accompanies the Paschal feast. Better still, we have become ourselves unleavened bread this 'new paste' which is none other than the new creation coming forth from the tomb with Christ:

'If then any man is in Christ, He is a new creature; the former things have passed away; behold, they are made new.'   *(II Cor. 5, 17; cf. Gal. 6, 15)*

Now, it is not a question of keeping any bit at all of the old leaven, there would be danger of fermenting the whole paste. The Jews used to take great care to sweep the whole house on the night of the thirteenth or fourteenth of the month Nisan, in order to clear out all trace of the leavened bread. We Christians must sweep our house also, as the Gospel tells us *(Lk. 11, 25)*, that is, clear out of ourselves and our fraternal community all malice and all impurity. Then, we shall celebrate worthily, in our whole life, the Paschal feast, where we have entered with Christ.

If we are a new creation, can we live like those who have not risen with Christ? Conversion to Christianity had been, for a few members of the Corinth community, a moral conversion. They had had to give up habits of debauch, then only too common in a pagan milieu. They had been very sincere converts, but, after some time, they were faced with many seductive temptations, in this vast cosmopolitan and libertine town. Certain ones were in danger of letting themselves fall back again. Worse still, they would gladly have allied moral licence with so-called spiritual principles. Nothing extraordinary in that: These towns where East and West met were often hives of sensual mysticism. Christianity was in constant danger of being contaminated by this taste for a troubled religiosity, conforming itself to depraved manners.

They went as far as using principles laid down by Paul himself. He liked to insist on Christian liberty: the Christian is freed, by Baptism, from sin and from wicked powers, he is liberated from the Law. Paul will develop these ideas at length when he will write to the Galatians and the Romans. Undoubtedly, he will use lapidary formulas like: 'Everything is permitted to me a Christian'. Like Saint Agustine, he will say later: 'Love, and do what you will'. Magnificent expressions of Christian liberty, but ones which have created ambiguity, in all times. That was indeed the case in Corinth and Paul reacted vigorously:

'All things are lawful for me, but not all things are expedient. All things are lawful for me but I will not be brought under the power of anyone. (...) Now the body is not for immorality but for the Lord, and the Lord for the body. Now God has raised up the Lord and will also raise us up by His power. Do you not know that your bodies are members of Christ?' *(6, 12-15, cf. 10, 23)*

In a few words all ambiguity is dissolved. Christian liberty? It exists, it is the fruit of Baptism, but we must not confound it with man's autonomy (personal freedom), still less with moral laxity. Christian liberty, is the restoration of a marvellous harmony between man, creation and God, thanks to Christ:

'For all things are yours, whether Paul, or Apollos, or Cephas; or the world, or life or death; or things present, or things to come – all are yours, and you are Christ's, and Christ is God.' *(3, 21-23)*

In this harmony man's body plays its part. Paul gives us here elements, which, though uttered rapidly in the course of his letter, are virtually, a rich and real theology of the body. More than one Christian in Corinth, confusing Greek philosophy with unsound mysticism, was, indubitably, making profession of despising the body under the pretext of valorising the mind. We shall find this problem cropping up again on speaking of the Resurrection. Paul protests energetically against this devalorisation of the body, which clashed with his profound knowledge of the Bible – and with his faith in Christ. Did not God create man soul and body? Does not the eminent dignity of the body appear

66

clearly in the corporal Resurrection of Christ?

Therefore, we have neither the right to despise our body nor to claim to use it as we wish. We belong to Christ: body as well as mind. Our body is for the Lord, because our whole being rose at Baptism, and it is destined to bear the image of the glorious Christ, on the day of the final Resurrection. And our Lord is for our body, because He is the source of the supernatural life which has already begun to transform our whole being; this transformation He continues in Eucharistic Communion.

How could we use as we like, this body which has become a member of Christ by the baptismal mystery? United to Christ as the wife is to her husband, should we claim to keep the free use of ourselves? Do we not belong to Him, henceforth, wholly for ever?

> 'Do you not know that your bodies are the temple of the Holy Ghost Who is in you, whom you have from God, and that you are not your own? For you have been bought at a great price. Glorify God and bear Him in your body.'   *(6, 19-20; cf. 3-16)*

In the correspondence that the Corinthians had exchanged with Paul, they had asked him his advice on marriage and on virginity. How should a Christian weigh these questions?

> 'It is good for man not to touch woman' *(7, 1).*

Such is Paul's spontaneous reaction. Yes, the Christian ideal changes notably the data of this problem, so deeply human. The Old Testament, so much aware of the grandeur of fecundity knew very little about the vocation to celibacy; only a few exceptional persons, like Jeremias, felt themselves called to it by God *(Jer. 16, 2).* Jesus revealed its mystery chosen deliberately for Him *(Mt. 19, 11-12).* Consequently Paul can write to the Corinthians:

> 'But I say to the unmarried and to widows, it is good for them if they so remain, even as I am.'   *(7, 7-8)*

Nevertheless, chastity remains, all the same, an affair of personal vocation. Paul does not for one moment think of making a rule about it. Christianity, which has revealed this superior vocation to the world, does not on that account devaluate marriage – far from that. In the *Letter to the Ephesians,* the union of husband and wife is represented as an image of the union of Christ and of the Church *(Eph. 5, 22).* God Himself has instituted marriage, and, as Christ recalled, He willed it indissoluble.

> 'But to those who are married, not I, but the Lord commands that a wife is not to depart from her husband, and if she departs, that she is to remain unmarried or be reconciled to her husband. And let not a husband put away his wife.' *(7, 10-11 : cf. Mt. 5, 32 and 19, 9)*

In a very simple, very direct manner, Paul lays down the Christian principle of the accomplishment of the marriage duty, the duty of husband and wife to each other:

> 'Let the husband render to the wife her due, and likewise the wife to her husband. The wife has not authority over her body, but the husband; the husband likewise has not authority over his body but the wife. Do not deprive each other except perhaps, by consent, for a time, that you may give yourselves to prayer; and return together again, lest Satan tempt you because you lack self-control.' *(7, 3-5)*

The celebrated text from Genesis: 'He created them man and woman... That is why a man shall leave his father and mother...' is evidently present all along this page to Paul's thought; in the same way our Lord had used it as a decisive argument against the Pharisees. The foundation of the whole doctrine of Christian marriage is an authentic sense of the creative work of God, of its sacred value, of the order which has to be respected in it.

It remains, that the concrete situation of the first Christians set special questions, which are still cropping up today, in mission countries, for example. Thus: either the husband or the wife is converted, the other remains a pagan. What is to happen then?

'To the others I say, not the Lord: If any brother has an unbelieving wife and she consents to live with him, let him not put her away. And if any woman has an unbelieving husband and he consents to live with her, let her not put away her husband. For the unbelieving husband is sanctified by the believing wife, and the unbelieving wife is sanctified by the believing husband.'

(7, 12-14)

The principle of indissolubility clearly imspires this answer of Paul. But also the conviction that each one of the spouses, is for his or her marriage partner, mediator of salvation. God's Design is to save each being by means of his fellow being, his neighbour. This plan of salvation finds its full realisation in the human couple who conform to the divine intentions.

It can certainly happen in the case considered by Paul, that the pagan partner wants a separation. As soon as this occurs, 'the brother or the sister' (the Christian partner) is no longer bound; 'because God has called you to live in peace' (7, 15). From the time of the Fathers of the Church, Christian tradition has always interpreted this text as authorising the Christian partner of the marriage to contract another marriage then. This is the 'Pauline privilege'.

At the end of this long and rich exposition on celibacy and marriage, Paul returns again to his personal ideal. The real, the only problem is to belong entirely to the Lord. Whoever does his duty 'in the condition which the Lord has allotted to each' (7, 17), married or celibate, (unmarried) does belong entirely to the Lord. However,

'I would have you free from care. He who is unmarried is concerned about the things of the Lord, how he may please God. Whereas he who is married is concerned

about the things of the world, how he may please his
wife; and he is divided.' (7, 32)

Neither for a Paul, nor for a Christian is there any question of refusing the corporal condition which is our present
state. But we must know how to find out, in the light of our
faith in the risen Christ, that our present state is only a
stage, a temporary realisation of God's Design. The
definite divine will is the glorification of man in his body
and in his soul: 'Even as we have borne the likeness of
the earthy, let us bear also the likeness of the heavenly'
(I Cor. 15, 49). At present, we are subject to many servitudes, those of the body, those of the heart; they prevent
us from belonging fully to God. But the person who gives
up marriage for the Kingdom of Heaven begins to be
liberated from a part of these servitudes, or, at any rate,
he transforms the sense of them. The power of the risen
Christ works more fully in his being and gives him a fore-
taste of the first fruits of the spiritual liberty of the world
to come.

Such an elevated Religious view does not at all prevent
Paul from being realistic. He shows this clearly in the
advice he gives a father concerning the marriage of his
daughter – it concerns the ancient paterfamilias who has
sovereign jurisdiction over the future of his children
(7, 36-38) – and to a widow about the question of re-
marriage (7, 39-40). Here again we see clearly the Apostle's
sense of the primacy of spiritual values. 'And I think that
I also have the Spirit of God' (7, 40)

Christian liberty is a great ideal; hence we must understand it thoroughly. Far from being freedom from the
moral law it is, we have just seen, submission to a superior
law, that of the world to come. Far from being the justification of individualism, it is the source of a better gift of
oneself to one's brothers, that is one's fellow-men. In his
Letter to the Galatians, Paul will write:

'For you have been called to liberty, brethren, But by
charity serve one another.' (Gal. 5, 13)

This problem of the relation between liberty and charity was one of those confronting the Church of Corinth.

The Corinthians found themselves in an embarrassing position as regards the sacrificing of meats to the idols. In a town as important as Corinth, public feasts and ceremonies were numerous; now, all these included sacrifices to the pagan divinities. The flesh of the sacrificed victims was consumed at sacred meals or sold in the town markets. What was a Christian to do? Could he eat these meats consecrated to false gods? Was he on the other hand to abstain rigorously from them?

Paul's answer is admirably firm and clear. Today, when the problem of idols and sacred meals no longer exists in our society, Paul's answer remains the safest guide to the use of Christian liberty. He understood perfectly, that the real question is that of the conflict of liberty and charity. Here is how he solves it:

> 'Now concerning things sacrificed to idols, we know that we all have knowledge. Knowledge puffs up, but charity edifies. If anyone thinks that he knows anything, he has not yet known as he ought to know. But if anyone loves God, the same is known by Him. *(8, 1-3)*

The problem is immediately raised to its proper level. It is characteristic of Paul to grasp immediately, the essential, though apparently trivial question at the heart of a debate. Knowledge and charity, there is the real question. The Corinthians boasted only too much of their spiritual knowledge; for them, religious life was above all a matter of knowledge: when one had knowledge one was a spiritual man, one was freed. We saw that Paul had already reacted severely in the first pages of his *Letter;* here, in one sentence, he demolishes Corinthian knowledge: 'If anyone thinks that he knows anything, he has not known as he ought to know', because real knowledge, that to which all Scripture and the whole life of our Lord bear witness, is love.

Having laid down this essential principle, Paul now makes the marvellous liberty of the Christian stand out in relief:

'Now as for food sacrificed to idols, we know that there is no such thing as an idol in the world, and that there is no God but one. For even if there are what are called gods, whether in heaven or on earth... yet for us there is only one God, the Father from Whom are all things and we unto Him; and one Lord, Jesus Christ, through Whom are all things, and we through Him.' *(8, 4-6)*

We are sovereignly free from the dominion of all the gods and of all the lords of paganism, because we know the only God and the only Lord. All comes from the Father through His Son; there is nothing, therefore, in the world which can hold us in slavery. On the contrary, every creature must help us to turn towards Christ and towards God. What matter to us, then, meats sacrificed to idols or other similar customs of pagan society?

'Now food does not commend us to God. For neither shall we suffer any loss if we do not eat, nor, if we do eat shall we have any advantage.' *(8, 8; cf. 10, 25)*

The profound liberty of the Christian cannot be more simply expressed.
But watch out! If we are conscious of this liberty and capable of using it, are others the same? Will not some of our weaker brothers be surprised and upset by it? Of course, Jesus did not hesitate to scandalise the Pharisees by His liberty towards Jewish customs; that was because He knew that their taking of scandal was pure affectation and self-interest. Paul himself scandalised more than once, by the newness of his doctrine; wherever the rights of truth, of the authenticity of the Gospel were concerned he could not remain silent. But he never scandalised by his conduct with respect to the Law, and in delicate circumstances, he emphasised respecting it and making it respected.[1]
Therefore, we have not the right to make such a use of

Author's Note: 1. See e.g. Ac. 16, 3.

liberty as would lead weaker consciences into error. We have not the right, in any free matter, to scandalise our brothers without a proportionately grave reason. We would be guilty towards them- and towards Christ Who died to save them.

> 'Still take care lest perhaps this right of yours becomes a stumbling-block to the weak (...) Now when you sin thus against the brethren and wound their weak conscience, you sin against Christ.' *(8, 9...12)*

And Paul concludes in a very spontaneous, very direct sentence, which bears witness to the absolute primacy of Charity:

> 'Therefore, if food scandalises my brother, I will eat flesh no more forever, lest I scandalise my brother.'
> *(8, 13; cf. Rom. 14)*

D. – *The witness of the apostle*

Paul wrote at the beginning of his *Letter:*
> 'I beg you be imitators of me.' *(4, 16)*

Not that he was conscious of having arrived at perfection, far from it. But he had such a sense of the greatness of his mission, of his responsibility towards Christ, that he spared nothing to acquit himself worthily of it. In that, he can dare to hold himself up as a model.
We speak about liberty. We saw that the Corinthians are very tempted to abuse Christian liberty. Paul will give them a good lesson: his own conduct on this point:

> 'Am I not free? Am I not an Apostle? Have I not seen Jesus, our Lord? Are you not my work in the Lord?'
> *(9, 1)*

The title of Apostle gives rights. Now, Paul is an Apostle

73

in the fullest sense of the word, and if some can deny it – Judaists, for example – it is certainly not the Corinthians who do so; he, alone is their 'father in Christ' *(4, 15)*.

The first right of the Apostle, is to receive the Apostle's salary. Would it be normal for him to be the soldier of Christ, the cultivator of the Lord's field, the pastor of His flock, without having the right to live by his work?

> 'What soldier ever serves at his own expense? Who plants a vineyard and does not eat of its fruit? Who feeds a flock and does not eat of the milk of the flock?'
>
> *(9, 7)*

Certain types of spiritual people, like some of those in Corinth, will think perhaps that this reasoning is very earthy, that the affairs of God cannot be evaluated by human computers. But God Who has made the earth, and Who put man on it to cultivate it, knows well that the labourer, in order to labour, must entertain hopes of the harvest, and that the reaper, in order to reap well, must entertain hopes for a share in the corn. That is true in every domain of man's work... It is profoundly human, and only too refined spiritual types can refuse to God the sense of the Human. His Law, however, bears witness to it on every page:

> 'Do you not know that they who minister in the temple eat what comes from the temple, and that they who serve the altar, have their share with the altar?' *(9, 13)*

Christ, also, continues Paul, 'directed that those who preach the Gospel should have their living from the Gospel' *(9, 14)*. Here Paul is certainly thinking of the following words of Jesus, which primitive tradition had taught him:

> ' (...) Remain in the same house, eating and drinking what they have; for the laborer deserves his wages.'
>
> *(Lk. 10, 7)*

Very well! However incontestable this right is Paul did not want to claim it. He renounced that liberty which apostolic custom and the very word of the Lord gave him. He preferred to earn his living working with his hands, so as not to be a burden to anyone. He did not want to accept any remuneration, so well did he understand that preaching the Gospel is for him an obligation from which he cannot withdraw.

'For woe to me if I do not preach the Gospel' (9, 16)

he cries, and this is but an echo of Jeremias:

'There came in my heart, as a burning fire shut up in my bones, I was wearied not being able to bear it.'

(Jer. 20, 9)

'What then is my reward?' continues Paul — 'That preaching the Gospel, I deliver the Gospel without charge, so as not to abuse my right in the Gospel.' (9, 18)

He joins thereto another word of Jesus, which does not contradict the first, but insists on the spirit of disinterestedness which must animate the Apostle:
'Freely you have received, freely give.' (Mt. 10, 8)
This is what the conduct of Paul was. So, let the Corinthians understand that before 'rights and liberty', there is charity! We must repeat here: 'I am allowed everything, but not everything is profitable.'
But go deeper still. Paul will reveal to us the secret of his apostolate, of every apostolate:

'For, free though I was, as to all, unto all I have made myself a slave that I might gain the more converts. And I have become, to the Jews a Jew that I might gain the Jews; to those under the Law, as one under the Law (though not myself under the Law) that I might gain those under the Law; to those without the Law, as one without the Law (though I am not without the Law of

75

God, but am undee the Law of Christ), that I might gain
those without the Law. To the weak I became weak,
that I might gain the weak. I became all things to all
men, that I might save all.'   (9, 19-22)

It is no question, here, of a method of propaganda which
consists in showing oneself to everyone to convert them to
one's own ideas; a compromise, or compromises, are
totally foreign to Paul's character. But he understood that
the cause of the Gospel would necessitate sacrifices – and,
in the first place, the sacrifice of oneself. He renounced
his independence, his ways of seeing and judging, to bring
himself down to the level of everyone in order to enter into
each one's psychology and adapt his preaching to it. For-
getfulness of oneself, of one's own views, of what we care
about most in the world, for the sake of the Gospel – there
is the secret of winning people to the Gospel.
Also, for the Apostle himself, it is the condition of his own
salvation. Because, after all would it not be ironically sad
if 'after preaching to others, I myself should be rejected'?
(9, 27). Paul is conscious of this danger and he wants
above all to make his Corinthians conscious of it. They
who are so sure 'of abounding in everything in faith, in
utterance, in knowledge, in all zeal' (II Cor. 8, 7), who
would so willingly give lessons to others, let them pay
attention to themselves!

'Do you not know that those who run in a race all indeed
run, but one receives the prize? So run as to obtain it.'
                                              (9, 24)

Games played a major part in the life of a city like
Corinth. Paul, always so near the real, sees in the games
of stadiums a very expressive image of Christian existence. We also run towards a goal, towards the crown of
glory which God promises to the conqueror. But who will
be conqueror? Nobody is sure of his eternal salvation.
Therefore, let us keep our eyes fixed on the object to be
attained, so as not 'to run without a purpose', that is, to

display efforts more spectacular than useful; and God knows that the Corinthians had a taste for the spectacular, in the religious life as well as everywhere else. Let us, the athletes of Christ, impose upon ourselves the necessary self-discipline, and let us not think 'everything is permitted;' he who cannot impose a severe discipline upon himself quickly becomes unfit for running!

'I so fight as not beating the air; but I chastise my body and bring it into subjection.'   (9, 26-27)

Upon the image of racing follows that of boxing. The idea remains the same; no useless fuss or excitement, let us aim at efficiency, real efficiency before God. Paul knew his Corinthians well; the advice he gives here must have stung them to the quick. He points out to this excessively effervescent community that it might get illusions concerning its real Christian efficiency. Of course, the Christian is free with regard to all things and all men; but the Apostle, who is freer than anybody else 'chastises his body and brings it into subjection'! The lesson is clear enough; let each one therefore examine himself; draw his own conclusions about himself and impose upon himself the necessary self-discipline.

E. – *The lessons of history*

'For I would not have you ignorant, brethren, that our fathers were all under the cloud, and all passed through the sea, and all were baptised in Moses, in the cloud and in the sea. All ate the same spiritual food, and all drank the same spiritual drink. Yet with most of them God was not well pleased, for 'they were laid low in the desert.'   (10, 1-5)

Immediately after the image of the stadium comes the story of Israel: a double evocation, of the Hellenistic world and of the Jewish people, which is very characteristic of

Paul. But Hellenism offered only one image; Israel presents us with figures, 'types', because such is the sense of the Greek terms employed here:

'Now these things came to pass as examples to us. Now all these things happened to them as a type.' *(10, 6...11)*

It is not by chance that Paul recalls the time of the Exodus. If the whole history of Israel is holy history, the Exodus is, par excellence, the gesture of God. If the whole history of Israel is that of salvation, the Exodus is, par excellence, the time of grace. Hence the Christian Church, from its very origins, recognised in the Exodus the exact type of the eschatological times in which it was living. Moreover, it took its inspiration from Jewish tradition; did not the rabbis all say that in Messianic times we would see the miracles of Exodus being renewed? When Saint John composed his *Gospel,* which recalls so many of the themes of the coming out of Egypt and of life in the desert: lamb, brazen serpent, running water, bread from heaven, etc., he only recalled and deepened this tradition. Therefore, we are not surprised to see Paul using the same typology for Christian existence.

Our Christian life is an Exodus, the new and definite Exodus. God has appointed and approved us a pilgrim people, by the grace of our baptism in water and in the Holy Spirit. We all march ever onward towards our Promised Land, this 'repose of God' into which we are invited to enter, as we read in the *Letter to the Hebrews.* To sustain us in our march, God feeds us with a supernatural food; to quench our thirst, He gives us the same supernatural drink; we all receive Holy Communion together and this tightens the bond of our unity: the sacrament of the Eucharist, that is the Body and Blood of Christ Himself, in the Mystery of the Passover, of His Exodus to which He associates us.

But take care! Let us not think that our salvation will be worked out without our co-operation. The merits of Christ are infinite, of course; but God asks the co-operation of our humble fidelity. So many graces can prove useless to us if we refuse this co-operation. The Israelites left us a fearful example: they also received a real baptism: 'in the cloud' which evokes the Spirit, and in 'the sea', the mystery of the water. They were approved by Moses, the chosen of God, as we ourselves are by Christ. They fed themselves on bread from heaven, they drank marvellous water from the rock. 'Now this rock was Christ.' Already, the Jewish theologians saw in the rock of the desert God Himself, Who in the *Psalms,* is so often called 'my rock' 'the Rock of Israel'. Paul, a Christian theologian educated in the school of the rabbis, recognises Christ in this miraculous stream, as the *Letter to the Hebrews* will recognise Him in the mysterious person of Melchisedech. Thus, Christ Himself, was already present in the Exodus from Israel: not, of course, in a sort of pre-Incarnation, but in so far as He alone is the principle of salvation for everyone. Throughout history God saves mankind by His Christ alone.

There is therefore no divergence between the history of Israel and ours. If at other times Paul highlights the opposition between the two covenants, the two Times, before Christ – in Christ, because this suits the Jewish mind, here, on the contrary, he insists on the unity of history. This suits the Greek mind better while still remaining deeply rooted in the biblical consciousness of the unity of the Design of God. His behaviour towards us today is no different from his behaviour towards the Israelites yesterday. So let us understand what He requires of us lest we be cast off like those 'who cannot enter into the rest of God *(Heb. 3, 19).*

Let us therefore, be vigilant, because we must all remember that 'if the spirit is willing, the flesh is weak' *(Mk. 14, 38).* But let us have confidence:

'God is faithful and will not permit you to be tempted beyond your strength, but with the temptation will also give you a way out that you may be able to bear it.'

(10, 13)

F. – *The meal of the Lord*

On several points the Church of Corinth was influenced by paganism. That is not at all astonishing in such a young community living in the heart of a pagan environment. Nevertheless, some of these influences constituted a real danger: this was noticeably the case in the celebration of the Eucharistic meal.

In fact, the religions of the Greco-Roman world had their sacred meals, also. Now, disorder often reigned in these celebrations which, sometimes, turned into an orgy. There was no thought about required moral dispositions. This threatened the contamination of the Christian Lord's Supper! It was Paul's duty to intervene:

> 'But in giving this charge, I do not commend you in that you meet not for the better but for the worse (...). When you meet together, it is no longer possible to eat the Lord's Supper. For at the meal, each one takes first his own supper, and one is hungry, and another drinks over-much.'
>
> *(11, 17-21)*

In a few words, Paul evokes the Corinthian assemblies in such a concrete way that we can easily get a picture of them in our minds. The first Christians used to celebrate the Eucharist during a meal, as Jesus Himself had done. But this meal should always have been deeply religious and fraternal; the Corinthians, however, used to take it without either order or dignity. Paul re-acted vigorously. However, he is not content with reforming abuses; as ever, he goes straight away to the essential data of the Christian faith. He will recall to the Corinthians the true sense of this Eucharistic Meal, which they seem to forget. In this way, he will give us a theological teaching of capital importance, which confirms and completes that of our Evangelists:

> 'For I myself, have received from the Lord (what I also delivered to you), that the Lord Jesus on the night on

which He was betrayed, took bread, and giving thanks broke, and said, 'This is My Body which shall be given up for you; do this in remembrance of me.'

In like manner also the cup, after He had supped, saying, 'This cup is the new covenant in My Blood; do this as often as you drink it, in remembrance of Me. For as often as you shall eat this bread and drink this cup, you proclaim the death of the Lord, until He comes.'

(*11, 23-26*)

The Eucharistic tradition is the very basis of the life of the Church. Paul wants to be one of its witnesses. When necessary, he stresses that he is giving his personal advice as an Apostle, which he did a little earlier (*7, 12-25*). He knows how to highlight his 'Gospel', that is, his knowledge of the mystery of Christ, as he did in the *Letter to the Galatians (1, 11)*. But here he only wants to transmit what he himself 'received' as *coming from the Lord,* because such is, very probably, the sense of the Greek preposition employed here. Paul was certainly instructed about the Eucharist following his conversion at Damascus. The Church transmitted to him the institution of the Lord's Supper, as he himself, in his turn, transmitted it to the Corinthians.

Therefore, he does not wish to teach them anything new. He only wants to remind them of the sense of the Lord's meal which they seem to have forgotten, judging from their behaviour.

Now, this Meal is the Sacrifice of Christ Himself. Paul, with Luke, kept for us the formula 'My Body (given, adds Luke) *for you*', which insists on the bond between the Last Supper and the Cross. He stresses this bond still more, by this very simple phrase, which is, however, a real theological commentary:

'Every time that you eat this bread and drink this blood, you announce the death of the Lord until He comes.'

The celebration of the Eucharist is the proclamation of the

death of the Lord Christ: proclamation, Messianic announcement, which is made by the accomplishment of the rite, and which is addressed, not only to the Christian, but to the whole of the human race, in order to teach it the capital event of its history. The Son of God was delivered for us, a victim fulfilling all the liturgical victims of the Ancient Covenant in His unique sacrifice. Paul evoked them, these victims of 'Israel according to the flesh', in one simple word which already prepares all the liturgical developments of the *Letter to the Hebrews (10, 18)*

This sacrifice of Christ is that of the New Covenant. It fulfills the prophecy of Jeremias:

> 'Behold the days shall come, saith the Lord, and I will make a new covenant with the house of Israel, with the house of Juda.' *(Jer. 31, 31)*

This New Covenant, like the first, is concluded in blood:

> 'Moses, we *read in the Book of Exodus,* took blood and sprinkled it on the people, saying: This is the blood of the Covenant which the Lord has made with you concerning all these words.' *(Ex. 24, 8)*

The Letter to the Hebrews, recalling all these texts, will show us the infinite superiority of the blood of Christ over the blood of the first Covenant, and, consequently, the transcendence of His Covenant over that of Moses.

Christ commanded His Church to renew this sacrifice. Here again, Paul and Luke explicitly recall this command of the Lord. It is clear, too, that Matthew and Mark were well aware of it, because the very first community in Jerusalem was already celebrating the Eucharist, as the book of the Acts testifies to us in the following passage:

> 'And they continued steadfastly in the teaching of the Apostles and in the communion of the breaking of the bread and in the prayers.' *(Ac. 2, 42)*

Paul, who wants to give its real value to the meal of the Lord in the Corinth community, brings into relief, Christ's intention in making the Supper His 'memorial' par excellence. Nevertheless, we must understand clearly the meaning of this memory. If the Greek term employed by Paul is of itself but a mere reminder of the past, we must not forget that it is laden here with all its biblical significance of 'memorial'. Now 'memorial', for the Israelite is much more than mere memory: it renders mysteriously present what it is meant to recall. Monument or rite, it has an efficacious character: just as the stone erected by Josue at Sichem, was a souvenir of the solemn promise of the people to God:

'Behold this stone shall be a testimony unto you that it has heard all the words of the Lord which he has spoken unto you.'   (Jos. 24, 27)

Now, among all the memorials mentioned in the Bible, there is one of exceptional importance: the Pasch.

'And this day shall be for a memorial to you: and you shall keep it a feast to the Lord in your generations with an everlasting observance.'   (Ex. 12, 14)

We read with reference to the day of immolation of the Paschal Lamb. As for the rite of the unleavened bread, closely bound up with the feast of the Pasch, we read:
'And it shall be as a sign in thy hand, and as a memorial before thy eyes: and that the law of Thy Lord be always in they mouth, for with a strong hand the Lord hath brought thee out of the land of Egypt.'   (Ex. 13, 9)

This double rite, of the lamb and of the unleavened bread is for Israel, all through its history, not only a reminder of the divine salvation granted formerly, but a permanent source of salvation. The rite renders divine intervention present. It makes man aware of it by making him remember the past; it renews it by making God remember His promises given to His people. The blood of the lamb, the rite of the unleavened bread, replace the tattooings which in the religions of the ancient Orient indicated belonging to God and, correlatively, His efficacious protection.

Jesus instituting the Eucharist repeated for us the command given formerly by God: that shall be as a memorial. The renewal of His sacrifice in the Church is no mere reminder of the past: its efficacious power of intercession in our favour is daily renewed in the countless Masses offered on the altars of the world. The Eucharist is for us on earth the anticipation of the Messianic feast to which Jesus invites all men. It is a call for the Return of Christ: 'until He return'... and already celebrates His victory and our salvation.

> 'Therefore whoever eats this bread or drinks the cup of the Lord unworthily, will be guilty of the body and the blood of the Lord. But let a man prove himself, and so let him eat of that bread and drink of the cup; for he who eats and drinks unworthily, without distinguishing the body, eats and drinks judgement to himself.'
>
> *(11, 27-29)*

The faithful Christian who communicates, unites himself really to Christ, victim of salvation. Paul does not insist on this reality of the body and blood of Christ in the Eucharist. He does not feel the need of reasoning or arguing to demonstrate it, because it is the very basis of his whole development. Consequently, he only recalls a teaching already given, which he considers understood by all in the community of Corinth, but neglected as to its consequences in life. The Corinthians celebrate the Eucharist in disorder, without suitable spiritual preparation, and in the church itself show their divisions! Are they then forgetting that the Eucharist is real participation in the Body and Blood of Christ?

> 'The cup of blessing that we bless, is it not the sharing of the Blood of Christ? And the bread that we break, is it not the partaking of the body of the Lord?' *(10, 16)*

How can we dare to approach this Bread and this Cup with a stained heart, which does not share the sentiments and the dispositions of Christ with Whom we want to be one? With a divided heart which would provoke 'the Lord to jealousy', as Israel did, formerly, in the desert? How can we dare approach Christ if we do not live in charity: this charity which is His first commandment, and of which He gives supreme testimony in His own Eucharist:

'Because the bread is one, we though many are one body, all of us who partake of the one bread.' *(10, 17)*

Eucharistic Communion, which deepens our union with Christ, sealed at Baptism, also deepens our union with all our brothers. With them we remain forever, one in Christ. In fact it is not a question of a simple fraternal meal; but of common participation in the unique Body of Christ.

G. – *Spiritual gifts*[1] *and the mystery of the Body of Christ*

The information that Paul received about the community of Corinth obliges him to intervene in another question: that of the gifts of the Holy Spirit, or spiritual gifts. Apparently a very different question from that of the Eucharistic Meal; in reality it will bring us to a new discovery of the Body of Christ.

Sensible manifestations of the Holy Spirit were frequent in the first Christian Churches; the book of the *Acts* retained numerous examples of them. They attested to believers that they had really entered, thanks to Jesus, into these Messianic times when God had announced that he 'would pour forth of His Spirit upon all flesh' *(Ac. 2, 17 quoting Joel 3, 1)*.

Spiritually gifted persons[2] were numerous in the Church of Corinth; that was a worry to Paul. Did not the Corinthians attribute too much importance to the exterior side

Translator's Note: 1. Original French: 'charismes'.
2. Charismatics.

of these spiritual graces, easily neglecting the interior work of the Spirit in souls? Had not they a tendency to assimilate these spiritual gifts to the manifestations of mysterious religions, very widespread in Corinth, and which a good number of Christians had been able to frequent before their conversion?

> 'Now, concerning spiritual gifts, brethren, I would not have you ignorant. You know that when you were Gentiles, you went to dumb idols according as you were led. Wherefore I give you to understand that no one speaking in the Spirit of God says 'Anathema' to Jesus. And no one can say 'Jesus is Lord,' except in the Holy Spirit.'
>
> *(12, 1-3)*

In these few words, Paul opposes in the strongest manner the attitude of the 'inspired' pagan to that of the authentic inspired Christian.

The definition of the inspired man, in the mysterious religions familiar to the Corinthians, is that he is a man led irresistibly by his ecstatic impulsions of the moment, no matter how abnormal or disorderly these are. The inspired man is passive, and, as it were under the absolute control of a constraining force. He pronounces words and does actions that have no relation to his real personality or to his normal psychology.

Now, there are in the Church of Corinth inspired persons who introduce into the assemblies the same type of 'mystical' phenomena. Under the impulsion of movements of which they are not masters, they go as far as cursing Jesus! Because Paul makes absolutely no allusion to Christians who would have apostasised. No, he wants to put the Corinthians on their guard against every suspect mystic. Words, attitudes which are in disaccord with the Christian faith, a fortiori, blasphemies, can be in their community, he tells them, but surviving traces of pagan mystique. If the community tolerates, and perhaps admires, these manifestations, on account of their strange and spectacular character, it is that it has not yet understood by what signs the presence of the Spirit is recognised. It takes for spiritual gifts what is only troublous mystique, pathological, perhaps even satanic.

Authentic Christian mysticism is quite different. It is not defined by spectacular phenomena but by the interior influence of the Holy Spirit on the man who opens himself up to His grace. The simplest act of faith and the truest, which consists in recognising with all one's soul, and in proclaiming before man, that 'Jesus is the Lord', is of the domain of grace; consequently it presupposes the action of the Spirit.

'For if thou confess with thy mouth that Jesus is the Lord, and believe in thy heart that God has raised Him from the dead, thou shalt be saved,'   *(Rom. 10, 9)*

Paul will write a little later in his *Letter to the Christians of Rome*.

Paul overthrew the hierarchy of values which pleased the Corinthians and which always seduce mankind so easily. The essentials of the mystic life are not spiritual phenomena but spiritual reality. Extraordinary spiritual gifts can therefore be shaded off in the continuation of the history of the Church. Reality remains, namely, faith, hope, charity, which bear witness, in all ages, to the interior action of the Holy Spirit.

'There are varieties of gifts, but the same Spirit; and there are varieties of ministries, but the same Lord; and there are varieties of workings, but the same God, Who works all things in all (...) All these things are the work of one and the same Spirit, Who allots to everyone according as He will.'   *(12, 4-6...11)*

Paul returns to the question of spiritual gifts. They must not be neglected now, under the pretext that they are not the essential of the Christian life. They are the gifts of the Spirit, consequently of authentic richness for the community. But they must be thoroughly understood.

Spiritual gifts are very diverse: Knowledge, miracles, prophecy, languages... There must be no sort of competition between inspired persons and the community must not be delivered over to disorder and to divisions: 'For God is a God of peace not of disorder' (14, 33). Let us understand this thoroughly: all these spiritual gifts find their unity in their source, which is the one and only Spirit, which is the Trinity, to which Paul here makes a discrete but certain allusion: same Spirit..., same Lord..., same God.

Now the Spirit, one and only source of spiritual gifts, destines them all for one end.

> 'Now the manifestation of the Spirit is given to everyone for profits.' (12, 7)

Thus, spiritual gifts are destined for the community, not at all for individuals. Paul insists on this point with an amused irony in regard to his Corinthians:

> 'But how, brethren, if I come to you speaking in tongues what shall I profit you, unless I speak to you either in revelation, or in knowledge, or in prophecy, or in teaching? Even inanimate instruments, like the flute or the harp, may produce sound, but if there is no difference in the notes, how shall it be known what is piped or harped? If the trumpet give forth an uncertain sound who will prepare for battle? (...) So, likewise you-, since you strive after spiritual gifts, seek to have them abundantly for the edification of the Church.' (14, 6-8...12)

And again, with respect to the gift of languages:

> 'For thou indeed, givest thanks well, but the other is not edified. (...) in the Church, I had rather speak five words with my understanding, that I may also instruct others, than ten thousand words in a tongue.' (14, 17-19)

All this page on spiritual gifts is charmingly vivacious and spontaneous, while at the same time it bears witness to the penetrating judgement of Paul in this infinitely deli-

cate domain of mysticism. All here is explained, simpli-
fied, and, finally, solved by his sense of the community.
Persons endowed with spiritual gifts are to the Christian
community what the Judges, the Prophets, the thauma-
turges or wonder-workers, were to ancient Israel. Spiritual
gifts are what miracles were in the Old Covenant, both in
the Church and, still more, in the earthly life of Jesus.
Witness of a presence, the sovereignly efficacious presence
of God, acting by His Spirit, in order to promote His people and transform the universe.

Here follows the capital teaching on this unity of the works
of the Spirit:

> 'For as the body is one and has many members, and all
> the members of the body, many as they are, form one
> body, so also is it with Christ.
> For in one Spirit we were all baptised into one body,
> whether Jews or Gentiles, whether slaves or free, and
> we were all given to drink of one Spirit.' *(12, 12-13)*

Here Paul uses a real parable: the parable of the human
body, which he develops at length in the following verses.
He did not borrow it from biblical tradition. It would be
useless our looking for this theme in the traditional images
of the Bible. The parables of the Bible and those of our
Lord, are borrowed from Palestinian nature: vine, harvest, trees, streams, rock, flocks... Perhaps we would find
in the literature of the Rabbis a few images borrowed
from the theme of the body, but they are very far from
having the character, the precision, and the development
which Paul gives it.
On the contrary, Greek literature, and especially that of
the Hellenistic epoch, likes to use the image of the body
and of its members as an expression of solidarity. We
have numerous examples of this among the Stoic writers.
In fact, Stoic morality and philosophy are founded on the
idea of solidarity: cohesion of the elements in the world,
solidarity of the men who share the same nature, the same

Logos, (that is Word or second Person of the Blessed Trinity), Who is the reason of the universe and the principle of its unity. Undoubtedly, it is from this Hellenistic milieu that Paul got the image of the body. But what doctrine does he make this image express?

One word resumes this doctrine:

'You are the Body of Christ.'   *(12, 27)*

An essential affirmation: so, it is not a question of a parable of the body only, of an image of the union of Christians between themselves, as we might think at the beginning. There is much more: the unity of Christians between themselves and with the Lord is such that they are identified with Christ: *you are His Body*.

A marvellous but upsetting revelation. How can we understand it?

What is certain is that the Corinthians themselves understood it. The facility, the simplicity, with which Paul speaks of it indicate sufficiently to us that the expression, like the doctrine, was already familiar to the Christians whom he had instructed. Better still, the expression the 'body of Christ' or simply the 'Body' was already probably the usual designation used by the Church. In any case, this will be so very clearly in the *Letters* of the captivity:

'He is the head of His body, the Church (...)' His Body, which is the Church...   *(Col. 1, 18-24)*
'God gave Him as head over all the Church, which indeed is His body...'   *(Ep. 1, 22-23)*
'Christ is Head of the Church, being Himself Saviour of the Body.'   *(Ep. 5, 23)*

But then, the expression 'Body', or 'Body of Christ' is a technical term and not at all an image! The data of the problem are inverted: it appears to us now that it is not the Hellenistic image which suggested the expression 'mystical body' of Christ; but it is the latter, familiar to the Christian community, which suggested the use of the parable of the members of the human body.

Yes! such appears indeed to have been the real proceeding: from the doctrine of the Body of Christ to the image of the human body, and not the opposite. Because, do not forget, that, from the origins of the Church, even before the conversion of Paul, the word 'body' is used chiefly in the theological sense: the Eucharistic sense. All the traditions of the New Testament formally agree: Jesus at the Last Supper, said 'My Body', and the Church, after Him, always repeated this same word.

Now is not the doctrine of the mystical Body, in this Letter, associated in a striking manner with Eucharistic faith?

'Because the bread is one, we, though many are one body.' *(10, 17)*

Eucharistic communion appears as the source of the unity of the mystical Body; believers constitute one single body, because they all participate in the body of Christ in the sacrament. The association of the two expressions is striking. The mystical body appears clearly as the fullness of the immolated and risen Christ, present in the Eucharist. Not that there is, as it were, an absorption of those who believe into Christ; nor that the personal Christ is blended with the community of those who believe. Every form of pantheism clashes radically with biblical and Christian thought. But there is a real extension of Christ to the Church: an extension of the mystery of the Incarnation.

This extension is conceivable only after the Resurrection of Christ and in virtue of this alone. Christ, having become 'spiritual' as St. Paul will say at the end of this *Letter* *(15, 44)*, is henceforth the principle, the 'head' of a new organism, really living with the life of the resurrection, an organism of which we are the members. The Church is thus the full physical reality of the risen Christ.

In the *Letter to the Galatians*, Paul will found the same doctrine of the mystical body of Christ on the mystery of our Baptism:

91

'For all you who have been baptised into Christ (...)
you are all one in Christ.'   *(Gal. 3, 27-28)*

Much more than a mere fraternal union is concerned:
'You are one', one single reality, one single being, or bet-
ter still, according to the expression of the *Letter to the
Ephesians:* 'one new man' *(Eph. 2, 15).*
Now Paul gives us the reason of this profound unity:

'You have put on Christ.'   *(Gal. 3, 27)*

Let us recall the realism of the words: a garment, 'to
put on,' in the Bible. The argument is the symbol of man
himself; to put on, that is to make one's own, to assimilate something to oneself, to identify oneself with a reality:
thus to 'put on justice, sanctity...' To put on Christ is therefore to assimilate oneself intimately to Him, to identify
oneself with Him. For we are all one new being in Christ,
because in baptism we identified ourselves with Him.
Baptism is then our incorporation in Christ. The Eucharist,
intimately connected with baptism, continually deepens,
enriches this identification. The realism of these two
sacraments indicates sufficiently that the expression mystical body is quite a different thing from an image. In these
sacraments of the Resurrection, we truly become the plenitude of the risen Christ.

H. – *The perfect way: charity*

In the mystical body of Christ, the different members
have different functions, according to the gifts of the Holy
Spirit:

'And God indeed has placed some in the Church, first
apostles, secondly prophets, thirdly teachers; after that
miracles, then gifts of healing, services of help, power of
administration, and the speaking of various tongues.'

(12, 27-28)

But these different spiritual gifts are of unequal value: not, certainly, from the point of view of their source, but from the point of view of the advancement of the community. The most spectacular are not always the most valuable. Paul wants to put the Corinthians on their guard against their taste for the sensational: since you so ardently desire the gifts of the Spirit, he says to them, 'strive after the greater gifts' *(12, 31)*.

But after all, there is, better still, a gift of the Spirit, more essential than all the others, that each Christian must desire:

> 'And I point out to you a yet more excellent way. If I should speak with the tongues of men and of angels, but do not have charity, I have become as sounding brass or a tinkling cymbal.
> And if I have prophecy and know all mysteries and all knowledge, and if I have all faith so as to remove mountains, yet do not have charity, I am nothing.' *(13, 1-2)*

This hymn to charity is for the community of the Corinthians a reminder of the essential of Christianity. As the simple act of faith 'Jesus is the Lord' is worth as much as the most spectacular spiritual gifts, so also charity alone constitutes the true value of a Christian in the eyes of God. Men rate very highly extraordinary mystical phenomena: the gift of languages, prophecies, the gift of miracles. But, after all, what is the Prophet or the worker of miracles worth, in the eyes of God? Much, if he lives in the grace of love; 'nothing', if he is not in His love.

The love which unites us to Christ, is, for Paul, the only reality that counts. He, who has the gift of languages 'I speak with all your tongues' *(14, 18)*, knows well that he is but a tinkling cymbal, if he does not live in the love of Christ. The hierarchy of spiritual values, which Paul continues to highlight from the beginning of this *Letter,* is most fully expressed here.

Besides, ought we not to judge everything with respect to

our final completion in Christ? Now, on the last day, the time of universal fulfilment,

> 'Prophecies will disappear, and tongues will cease, and knowledge will be destroyed. But 'charity never fails'.'
> *(13, 8)*

The Spirit multiplies spiritual gifts in His Church to give to the Body of Christ, and to each one of His members, the means of reaching the perfection for which God destines him. But spiritual gifts marked with the imperfection of this world, will no longer have any reason for existing once this perfection is attained.

> 'When that which is perfect has come, that which is imperfect will be done away with.' *(13, 10)*

Man, become adult, abandons the ways of knowing, of judging and of acting that he had as a child. The same thing will happen to the baptised person. When he will reach the full bloom of his baptismal life, having attained 'to perfect manhood, to the mature measure of the fullness of Christ' *(Eph. 4, 13)* in the mystical Body, then all the imperfect modes of knowledge which are his in the present world, will disappear. Charity alone will remain, charity which is perfect 'knowledge', because it is communion.

> 'We see now through a mirror in an obscure manner, but then face to face. Now I know in part, but then I shall know even as I have been known. So there abide faith, hope, and charity, these three; but the greatest of these is charity.' *(13, 12-13)*

To the Corinthians, eager for religious knowledge and mystical contemplation, Paul recalls that there is no real knowledge except in love, no real vision except in communion. Such was already the message of the Prophets, of Osee in particular:

'I will espouse thee to me... in mercy and in commis-
serations. I will espouse thee to me in faith: and thou
shalt know that I am the Lord.'   (Os. 19-20)

Such will be the message of John, in his *Gospel* and in his
Epistles:

'Everyone who loves knows God, He who does not love
does not know God, for God is love.'

(I Jn. 4, 7-8)

The whole Christian theology of knowledge is there.

I. – *The mystery of the Resurrection*

In the Church of Corinth Christians are to be found who
doubt the resurrection of the dead. Not the Resurrection of
Christ Himself, which is the first affirmation of the Christian faith, but the general resurrection of the dead, at the
Return of Christ. How could believers come to this heresy,
for, after all it is a heresy? Paul's answer tells us how. If
these Christians doubt the Resurrection or even deny it,
it is for philosophic reasons. They have had too much difficulty in conceiving its possibility and its manner. The
'how' escapes them, and this insurmountable difficulty
brings them to refuse it.
According to all available evidence, these Christians are
'sages' in the sense of the first pages of this *Letter*. They
want to understand the mystery, they ask to have the resurrection explained and justified to them. Influenced by
Greek spirituality, they grasp neither the possibility nor
even the sense of the resurrection of the body. Hasn't
Paul met this difficulty before in Athens?

'Now when they heard of a resurrection of the dead,
some began to sneer, but others said, 'We will hear thee
again on this matter'.'   (Ac. 17, 32)

So, once more, Paul meets human wisdom in conflict with the Gospel of Christ. To answer it he will develop a veritable catechetics of the Resurrection one of the most beautiful that we have in the New Testament.

> 'For I delivered to you first of all, what I also received, that Christ died for our sins according to the Scriptures, and that he was buried and that he rose again the third day, according to the Scriptures, and that he appeared to Cephas and after that to the eleven. Then he was seen by more than five hundred brethren at one time, many of whom are with us still, but some have fallen asleep. After that he was seen by James, then by all the Apostles. And last of all, as by one born out of due time, he was seen also by me.' *(15, 3-8)*

What simplicity and what strength in this sequence of affirmations! This text is not exactly Pauline; indeed here, it is rather the reminder of a paschal catechetics already known by the Corinthians, because it belonged to the common fund of Primitive catechetics, from which all the Apostles, Evangelists and founders of churches drew. Here Paul is, and wishes to be merely an echo of the tradition of the Christian community. This Primitive catechetics imposed itself on all, even on a genius as personal as Paul: 'For I delivered to you first of all what I also received'. On this essential point of the resurrection, as on that other which is the Eucharistic doctrine, Paul only wishes to know 'what he has received' *(11, 23)*.

He transmits to us therefore the witness of the Church to the Resurrection of Christ. We say rightly: the witness of the Church. It it not a matter of a set of individual unconnected witnesses. In reality, it concerns different aspects of one unique witness. The apparitions mentioned are significant: to Peter, the head of the Church – to the Twelve, on whom Christ wanted to found the Church – to a group of five hundred brethren, evidently representing the whole community of believers – to James, head of the Mother-church in Jerusalem – at last, and this is the only personal element of this witness, to Paul himself, the Apostle of the Gentiles. It is therefore the whole Church which bears witness to the Resurrection and the heavenly exaltation of Jesus. Since its origin, and throughout its history, the Church continues to be 'witness of His resurrection' *(Ac. 1, 22)*.

Moreover this witness is only valid, because the witness of God is joined to it. God bears witness to his envoy, by His own Word, contained in the Holy Scriptures. The Church, rereading these Scriptures in the light of Christ, discovers, there the proclamations of the mystery of the death and resurrection. This discovery, made in faith, is the last source of the witness which the Church bears to her Christ, to bring about 'obedience to faith' *(Rom. 1, 5)*, among all the nations.

Thus this witness is at once historic, for it bears indeed on a fact of our history – juridical, because it lends itself to inquiry and discussion – and theological, because it is spread by believers to promote and advance the faith. It is infinitely more profound and more rich than mere human witness which is only a pale image of it. Hence it can be, today as yesterday, the very basis of the Christian community, for

'If Christ has not risen, vain then is our preaching, vain too, is your faith.' *(15, 14)*

'Now if Christ is preached as risen from the dead, how do some among you say that there is no resurrection of the dead? But if there is no resurrection of the dead, neither has Christ risen.' *(15, 12-13)*

This for Paul is the first truth, the answer to all the difficulties raised by the Corinthians: the Resurrection of Christ involves ours. If we admit the former, we must also admit the latter. This involvement implies an essential coherence of the faith, which the Corinthians are in danger of forgetting, and which Paul wants them to realise. Christ carries us along with Him and calls us to pass through His own mysteries:

'Christ has risen from the dead, the first fruits of those who have fallen asleep. For since by a man came death, by a man also comes Resurrection of the dead.

For as in Adam all die, so in Christ all will be made to live. But each in his own turn, Christ as first-fruits, then they who are Christ's who have believed at His coming.'
(15, 20-23)

These few phrases give us the whole essential of the Pauline theology of the Resurrection. Christ is Himself 'first-fruits' of those who died; this very beautiful image evokes immediately for us the first fruits of the crops and of the harvests, which the Jewish Law declared sacred and belonging to God: their offering at the sanctuary called down the divine benedictions on the land of Israel. Christ is first-fruits, because He is the first risen, the chief, the head of the mystical body, all of whose members are called to rise with Him. In another *Letter*, Paul will give to Christ another name which means the same thing: 'first-born from the dead' *Col. 1, 18; cf. Apoc. 1, 5)*, and he will add: 'that in all things He may have the first place.' These last words are clear enough: it is the doctrine of the mystical body which dominates the whole theology of the Resurrection. If Christ is risen, we are all called to rise with Him, because, from the time of our Baptism, we form with Him but one single being. Our destiny is henceforward inseparable from His; and already, in His Resurrection, ours begins to be accomplished:

'God has raised us up together with Him (Christ) and seated us together in heaven.' *(Eph. 2, 6)*

as St. Paul will write later to the Christians of Ephesus.

The parallel with the first man, Adam, gives a still greater insight into this theology of the mystical body. Paul will return to it towards the end of this same page, and he will develop it completely in his *Letter to the Romans (5, 12-21)*.

This parallel, in fact, is at the same time an opposition.

98

Humanity, and with it the whole of creation, has two successive heads: Adam, in the beginning of time; Christ, at the end of time. The one, like the other, a chief named by God, a lord of creation, a head of humanity, draws along all men in his own destiny. Now that of Christ is the glorious resurrection and life, the reward, as the *Letter to the Romans* will tell us, of His obedience. 'All die in Adam; all will live again in Christ.'

But we do not all enter immediately into this world of the resurrection where Christ has already entered. That is because the Design of God unfolds itself throughout the march of time, in the continual warfare between the powers of death and the powers of life. Christ Himself led this war; apparently conquered at the time of the Crucifixion, He finally triumphed on Easter morning. We also have to wage this war until the day fixed by God. Then 'comes the end' when 'the last enemy, death' will be definitely destroyed *(15, 24-26)*. The work of death of the first man, Adam, will have been superabundantly repaired by the work of the last man, Christ, and 'we will reign in life, through the one Jesus Christ' *(Rom. 5, 17)*.

Paul established the dogma of our resurrection, by attaching it entirely to the fact of the resurrection of Christ. He hopes he has convinced the Corinthians; but he knows that grave difficulties exist, and he does not want to steal away from them:

'But someone will say 'How do the dead rise? Or with what kind of body do they come?' *(15, 35)*

Some Christians of Corinth who either were or thought themselves to be 'philosophers', put forward that type of objection, typical of the intellectuals. It is as difficult to conceive the resurrection on the scientific as on the philosophic plane. The sages of this world, those who want to explain everything rationally, here collide with an almost insurmountable difficulty.

Paul will answer them, however. To these intellectuals, he

99

will present an explanation. He does not claim to suppress the mystery; but he will show us that this mystery is similar to other mysteries, familiar to us, which we meet every day without showing any surprise at them. The resurrection of bodies is part of a general order willed by God, inscribed in the midst of the very universe in which we live.

> 'Senseless man, what thou thyself sowest is not brought to life, unless it dies. And when thou sowest thou dost not sow the body that shall be, but a bare grain, perhaps of wheat or something else. But God gives it a body even as He has willed, and to each of the seeds a body of its own.'
> *(15, 35-38)*

'Senseless man' shouts Paul to the sage who makes objections. But of course, how is it that this so-called sage cannot read, in the simplest and most familiar fact of the seed become a plant, a veritable parable of the resurrection! Because that is what it is, and Paul, like Jesus Himself when He was revealing the secrets of the Kingdom, invites us to pay attention to the mystery of the seed.

In it we discover a law: that of the passage, through death, to a new form of life.

In fact, in the fate of the grain of seed thrown into the earth, we see that death can be a source of life and even that it is normally the trial through which we must pass to reach the plenitude of life. This Jesus Himself tells us in the Gospel:

> 'Unless the grain of wheat falls into the ground and dies, it remains alone; but if it dies it brings forth much fruit.'
> *(Jn. 12, 24)*

But the life that we enter through death is no longer the same as it was formerly; it is still a corporal life, but the corporal life that preceded it can give scarcely any idea of it. The seed has become a plant or a tree, it now possesses an infinitely different and an infinitely richer existence than before.

So also will it be with us. Paul does not apply the parable, but we can do so easily. The resurrection will give us a body, but our present body can give us no idea of what kind of body this will be. Because the corporal realities that we know do not exhaust the concept of the body; or rather, they do not exhaust the creative power of God. Such was already the answer of Jesus to the Sadducees, who were denying the resurrection:

> 'You err because you know neither the Scriptures nor the power of God (...) For at the resurrection they will be as angels of God in heaven.'   *(Mt. 22, 29-30)*

Like the angels of God... Jesus did not wish to say that we become entirely spiritual beings; but that our corporal life will be profoundly spiritualised: 'they will neither marry nor be given in marriage' – and that we shall no longer labour under the habitual laws of the bodily life that we know here below.

And now Paul proposes a second parable which prolongs the preceding one. It is the parable of the diversity of bodies:

> 'All flesh is not the same flesh, but there is one flesh of men, another of beasts, another of birds, another of fishes.'   *(15, 39)*

Yes, in the world in which we live, we can already observe a multiplicity of bodies, of 'fleshes' as Saint Paul says. In fact, whether speaking of man, or of animals, or of birds or of fish we say that they have a body, a 'flesh'. But no one will deny that these fleshes are of a different nature; let us be more precise: of a different perfection. So we would be very wrong, when thinking of 'body' to think only of our present body. Many other possibilities are undoubtedly open.

Let us enlarge on the observation. Let us look at it from the scientist's point of view – science at the time of Paul. What does it teach us?

'There are also heavenly bodies and earthly bodies, but
of one kind is the glory of the heavenly, of another kind
the glory of the earthly. There is one glory of the sun,
and another glory of the moon, and another of the stars;
for star differs from star in glory.'   *(15, 40-41)*

Thus the whole universe reveals, in the most glorious manner, the infinite variety of corporal substances, and with
this the infinite possibilities of the creative power of God.
Does the dogma of the resurrection astonish us? That is
because we do not fully realise the almighty power of
God. However, the universe is there all around us, in its
infinite diversity. This already teaches us all the creative
richness of the action of God. By taking the trouble to
understand this teaching thoroughly, we shall come to
understand the resurrection itself. It will be easy to see in
it, not a unique and extraordinary miracle, but the definite
manifestation of the presence of God, and the completion
of the mystery of Creation.
Paul, having done all this, did not claim to 'prove the resurrection. But he permits us to grasp its sense and value
by situating it in the universal order of the divine Design,
by making us recognise in it the crowning of the creative
work of God.

The two parables that Paul proposed to us: the parable of
the passage through death to a new life, the parable of the
diversity of corporal substances, permit us to enter now
into the mystery of the resurrection.

'So also with the resurrection of the dead. What is sown
in corruption rises in incorruption; what is sown in dis-
honour rises in glory; what is sown in weakness rises
in power; what is sown a natural body rises a spiritual
body.'   *(15, 42-44)*

Consequently, it will be with us as with the grain of seed
thrown into the earth. Between our present body and our
risen body, will intervene a profound transformation, a

veritable transfiguration. We shall pass from the 'natural' order to the spiritual order, that is from a body of flesh and blood, marked by the weaknesses and the limitations of its members and senses, to a body penetrated by the spirit, in perfect harmony with the soul which, transparent to this presence of the Spirit, will be governed completely by Him. Our whole being will belong to the heavenly world and will bear its image. That is why we shall be 'as angels of God in heaven' *(Mt. 22, 30).*

In fact, Paul affirms,

'What is sown a natural body rises a spiritual body.'

(15, 44)

This time, it is no longer a parable that Paul proposes to us; he formulates a real law. He does not free it from the observation of the created world; for it belongs to the metaphysical order, and more precisely still, to the order of revelation, even if its formulation can be borrowed from some philosophy or mystique of that time.

In fact, it is explained by a text from Scripture, whose development will clarify the last and richest aspect of this theology of the resurrection:

'So also it is written, 'The first man, Adam, became a living soul'; the last Adam became a life-giving spirit. But it is not the spiritual that comes first, but the physical, and then the spiritual. The first man was of the earth, earthy; the second man is from heaven, heavenly. As was the earthy man, such also are the earthy; and as is the heavenly man, such also are the heavenly. Therefore, even as we have borne the likeness of the earthy, let us bear also the likeness of the heavenly.' *(15, 45-49)*

Hence, starting from the Text of *Genesis*, Paul evokes again – he has already done so at the beginning of this page – the theme of the two men in whom the whole destiny of our humanity is fulfilled.

God did not create one man, but two. Each one really deserved to be called man, because each was, by himself, the representative of the whole human race. One appears at the beginning of time; the other at the beginning of the eschatological era.

Therefore we are confronted with a real dualism, since each one of these two men represents the whole human race. But this dualism is finally solved, according to biblical tradition, in unity. We will see this unity, if we can recognise, in these two men the succession of two orders, in which the second must finally absorb the first. First comes the earthy, or natural, or carnal order of the first creation and the first Adam. Then follows the heavenly or spiritual order manifested in Christ who 'comes from heaven' by His Incarnation. Saint John in his *Gospel* tells us in very similar terms:

'He who is from the earth belongs to earth (...) He who comes from Heaven is over all.'   *(Jn. 3,31)*

Now this succession of the two 'men', and in them of the two orders of creation, indicates clearly enough for us that the history of salvation proceeds from the imperfect to the perfect. Therefore God wants to teach us also to accept this mysterious passage from the imperfect to the perfect, from a life full of earthly contingencies to a superior life. We must belong to this deficient humanity, before belonging to a glorious humanity. We work out in our personal destiny this succession of the two orders which revelation teaches us.

As in his *Letters to the Thessalonians,* Paul considers the return of Christ in the near future. Hence he can write:

'(...) We shall not all sleep but we shall all be changed.'   *(15, 51)*

We have no longer, today, the same sense of the proximity of the return of Christ as the first Christian generation had. But the essential affirmation of Paul remains still valid.

'(...) We shall be changed. For this corruptible body must put on incorruption, and this mortal body must put on immortality.' *(15, 52-53)*

Like the risen Christ, we must become spiritual and heavenly. Animated by this ardent hope, Paul concludes by a cry of triumph:

'Then shall come to pass the word that is written: Death is swallowed up in victory.' *(15, 54)*

3

Greatness and Weakness of the Apostle of Christ

The Second Letter to the Corinthians

The circumstances in which Paul wrote this *Second Letter to the Corinthians* are much less clear to us than those in which he wrote the *First*.

Paul was often in touch with the Church of Corinth and the relations between the two are often confused enough. The most likely circumstances are as follows:

After having written his so-called *First Letter to the Corinthians* (it is really the second) Paul learns that new difficulties have arisen in the community. Judaising preachers, from no one knows where, attack, in their sermons, his person, his character, his apostolic authority. So, Paul writes to the Christians of Corinth a letter, now lost, but which we know about from certain allusions in our '*Second to the Corinthians*'. This sorrowful and indignant Letter provokes a lively emotion in the community and restores a little calm.

Meanwhile, Paul left Ephesus as a result of the gold-smiths' riot. He reached Macedonia through Troas and headed for Greece. In Macedonia, Titus brings him news of the Corinth community. It is then that he writes our *Letter,* to announce his own arrival. It is probably the year 57 A.D.

The authenticity of this *Letter* is not contested; and indeed the ideas, the language, the style are Pauline, in the strictest sense of the term. But as is the case in the *First to the Corinthians*, people discuss the unity of this *Letter*. The absence of transition between one subject and another, divergencies of views in the course of the *Letter*, on one and the same subject or on analogous subjects, undeniably pose many questions.

In particular, chapter 9 on the collection, resumes in an entirely different perspective the theme of chapter 8. Chapters 10 to 13 which constitute the celebrated 'apologia' of Paul, are singularly different from the preceding chapters by the vivaciousness, the very violence so to speak, of their style. We have reason to believe that in these two cases we are dealing with pages written by Paul, pages which did not in the beginning form part of this *Second Letter to the Corinthians*. Chapter 9 was probably written to some community in Achaia, and was later inserted in the Letter addressed *to the Corinthians*. As to the apologia of chapters 10 to 13, it was indeed written to the Church of Corinth, but in circumstances different from those of our Letter. Moreover it is very difficult to specify these circumstances.

Let us remember in any case that these observations represent no attack on the Pauline character of our *Letter*. Among all the epistles it will even seem to be the most personal, the most vibrant, the most revealing of the heart and soul of Paul.

A. – *Trials and consolations*

Paul has just passed through a terrible trial, which profoundly affected him. Moreover it does not concern his worries about the Corinth community, but a precise event which endangered his life and crushed him for a while.

> 'For we would not, brethren, have you ignorant of the affliction which came upon us in Asia. We were crushed beyond measure – beyond our strength, so that we were weary even of life. Yes, we have been carrying within our very selves, our death sentence...' (*1, 8-9*)

Does Paul intend to tell us about the riot of the goldsmiths of Ephesus, described in the Acts (*Ac. 19, 23*)? Not at all, because he was not in danger of death there. It concerns another event, very probably a serious illness of his rather than a persecution; because, he tells us in a realistic manner, he has been 'carrying within his very self' his death sentence. We know that Paul had been seriously ill when he was evangelising the Galatians, about the year 50

(Gal. 4, 13-15). Possibly he had recently suffered a particularly serious and painful bout of his chronic infection –
probably one of the fevers.

Does his having been crushed mean that he feared death
so much? Certainly not... He himself will tell us a little
further on that 'while we are in the body we are exiled
from the Lord', and that he would prefer 'to be exiled from
the body and to be at home with the Lord' *(5, 6-8).* A few
years later he will write to the Christians of Philippi:

> 'For me to die is gain (...). I desire to depart and to be
> with Christ, a lot by far the better.'   *(Phil. 1, 21-23)*

No, Paul was not afraid of death. He aspired too much to
perfect union with Christ to fear this painful passage. But,
in this trial which came upon him in Asia, his body, his
whole being was a prey to sufferings which must have
been accompanied by states of complete annihilation. In
these moments of prostration, when death seemed near,
Paul had the impression that his work of evangelisation
was going to remain unfinished, that God was asking him
to give up all the apostolic plans that he had formed. As
Apostle of the pagan world, he had still so much to do!
God, Who had sent him was recalling him suddenly, before he had accomplished his mission. That is what was
torturing Paul. His submission to the divine will did not
prevent his being overcome by mortal agony.

But now in the depths of this agony, he has an extraordinary experience: that of divine consolation. This made
such a profound impression on him that God is now for
him 'the God of all consolation'.

> 'Blessed be the God and Father of our Lord Jesus Christ,
> the Father of mercies and the God of all comfort, Who
> comforts us in all our afflictions, that we also may be
> able to comfort those who are in any distress. For as the
> sufferings of Christ abound in us, so also through Christ
> does our comfort abound.'   *(1, 3-5)*

God of consolation! That is exactly how God had revealed Himself to His people Israel, in the darkest days of the Exile:

'Be comforted, be comforted my people, saith your God.' *(Is. 40, 1)*

'The Lord hath comforted His people...' *(Is. 49, 13)*

'I, I myself will comfort you...' *(Is. 51, 12)*

The consolation reveals all the love, paternal love, better still, maternal love of God for Israel:

'As one whom the mother caresseth
So will I comfort you
And you shall be comforted in Jerusalem.' *(Is. 66, 13)*

Paul, in the night of trial, had this same experience. But, in the light of his Christian faith, suffering like consolation, is clothed in a new meaning. Suffering? Can it be anything else but a participation in the Passion of Christ? In us it is a prolongation of the sufferings of our Saviour; these 'overflow' as Paul almost says, upon us, the members of his body. It is the vocation of the baptised person 'what is lacking of the sufferings of Christ, I fill up in my flesh for His body' *(Col. 1, 24)*.

In the same way consolation is the sign of our communion with Christ. It is from Him, 'consolation of Israel' *(Lk. 2, 25)*, and from Him alone, that we receive henceforward all consolation. Did not He proclaim Himself:

'Blessed are those who weep, for they will be comforted.' *(Mt. 5, 4)*

Henceforth, the believer knows that he owes all comfort, all joy, all consolation, to the mediation of Jesus alone. Just as our suffering is the prolongation of the Passion of Christ in us, so also consolation is the prolongation of the joy and of the glory of the Resurrection. In the midst of suffering, we learn:

> 'In order that we may not trust in ourselves, but in God who raises the dead. He it is who delivers us, from such great perils.' *(1, 9-10)*

Consolation is in our life an experience of the light of Easter. It makes us feel the power of God, that very power which delivered Christ from the darkness of death. It is, in us, anticipation of this glorious resurrection towards which our baptism launches us.

Hence the Apostle cannot keep for himself this joy of consolation. He knows that it is not a personal euphoria but a comfort for all the members of the mystical body. Together we share in the sufferings of Christ; together we are to taste the final consolation of the Resurrection. This divine comfort is therefore a common fund from which we all draw support and encouragement. The suffering Christ, the consoling Christ dwells in each one of us. None of our states is indifferent to the Church of Christ:

> 'And if one member suffers anything, all the members suffer with it, or if one member glories, all the members rejoice with it.' *(I Cor. 12, 26)*

More than anybody else, the Apostle feels himself intimately united to the Christian community. He realises, in an exceptional degree, that he has received nothing for himself alone. Through him, God plans all things: success and failure, suffering and joy, for the Church of Christ. Through him comes about the communion of all men in the mysteries of Christ. Consequently he can affirm to his Christians:

> 'And our hope for you is steadfast, knowing that as you are partakers of the sufferings, so will you also be of the comfort.' *(1, 7)*

B. – *The apostolate, service of truth*

Paul had many difficulties with the Church of Corinth, especially in the period which preceded this *Letter*. He has to handle these painful subjects, and focus whatever is necessary. His character and methods are criticised, his intentions suspected. He has to defend himself. But is he going to polemise? No, he has too much greatness of heart and of mind to lower himself to that. He will deliver over to us, in the simplest, the most personal, the most direct way, 'the testimony of his conscience'; and into this witness passes his entire conception of the apostolate.

> 'For our boast is this, the testimony of our conscience that in simplicity and godly sincerity – not in carnal wisdom but in the grace of God – we have conducted ourselves in the world, and especially in our relations with you.' *(1, 12)*

Carnal wisdom is conduct inspired by purely human feelings and using means of success suggested by human ingenuity. They reproach Paul for doing this. But he knows well, what motives inspire his action and what methods he uses to conquer men and make them submit to Christ. Being a fervent Jew he knew already that the ways of God are not those of men and that His thoughts are not our thoughts; for such is the message of all the Prophets and of the whole Bible. When he became a Christian he entered fully into the Mystery of the designs of God: this mystery which reveals the Cross to us. Since then, he penetrated deeper and deeper into the mystery, making it, ultimately pass into his own life. His meeting with the Greek world in Athens, even in Corinth, made him grasp with a new intensity, this paradox of the Wisdom of God, scandal and folly for the wisdom of man. Was not that the very subject of his *First Letter to the Corinthians*? Those who accuse him of acting from motives inspired by human wisdom have no understanding of his religious experience. This experience, from the moment of his vocation, was that of the grace of God. Henceforward, he no longer wants to think, act, live for any other reality than that. To be transparent to grace, to deliver himself up to its action, to bear testimony only to its inspiration and its presence, such is the ideal of his apostolic life. That is what he calls: 'simplicity and godly sincerity in the grace of God.' It is not a question of a human loyalty only; but of loyalty to grace. The apostle is really in the service of truth when he wants to be only the faithful instrument of the mystery of the grace of God.

Paul had planned to pass through Corinth first, to go from there to Macedonia, then to return to Corinth and to embark from there for Judea *(1, 15-16)*. Circumstances did not permit him to carry out this plan. But he had already told the Corinthians about it; they were disappointed and undoubtedly somewhat vexed. Paul's enemies took advantage of this to insinuate criticism: was not this Paul a tormenting queer fellow, always announcing great plans and never carrying them out? What confidence could anyone have in him? With him, nobody could ever be sure of anything!
Paul answers these insinuations vivaciously:

'Now in this my intention, did I show fickleness? Or are my plans made according to the flesh, so that with me it is now 'Yes' and now 'no'? God is my witness that our message to you is not both 'yes' and 'no'. For the Son of God, Jesus Christ, who was preached among you by us – by me and Silvanus and Timothy – was not now 'yes' and now 'no', but only 'yes' was in him. For all the promises of God find their 'yes' in Him; and therefore through Him also rises the 'Amen' to God unto our glory.' *(1, 17-20)*

It is only Paul who can thus elevate the most human debate to the plane of divine realities. They reproached him with a lack of continuity, perhaps even of sincerity, in his ideas. He answers by appealing to the constancy and sincerity of Christ. The Son was not 'now' 'Yes' and now 'no'; he sought no compromise between the will of the Father and human success, as the Tempter suggested to Him. He wanted to know nothing except the will of God alone. That is why all the prophecies are fulfilled in Him. In His Christ, God said yes to men, granting them definitely what he had promised them centuries ago. Therefore in their turn, men answer yes to God in Christ, the Mediator of all prayer. In Him and through Him, they acclaim the universal work of salvation of God, when they pronounce the Amen of the Christian liturgy. This we have already seen in the First *Letter to the Corinthians:*

'How shall he who fills the place of the uninstructed say 'Amen' to thy thanksgiving? For he does not know what thou sayest.'   *(I Cor. 14, 16)*

In the Christian churches, they already had the habit of answering Amen to the prayers made by a member of the community in the name of all. Moreover, it was the custom in the synagogues, and the Old Testament itself offers us several examples of the same thing. Amen was the engagement of the grateful community, making its own the words just read or pronounced; from whence Paul's remark, that one cannot say Amen, that is engage oneself, on what one had not understood.

From the outset we know that Christian prayer was addressed to God through Christ; and there is no doubt that a formula analagous to our 'through our Lord Jesus Christ' – 'Amen' was used in the early Church. Thus Christ is at once the Amen of God to man, the Amen of man to God. Do we not read in the *Apocalypse* of St. John:

'Thus says the Amen the faithful and true witness, who is the beginning of the creation of God...' *(Apoc. 3, 14)*

Very well. Can the Apostle, envoy of Christ, representative of Christ among men, be different from His master? Can one imagine in him, 'now 'Yes', now 'No',' compromises of the duplicity which human ingenuity teaches? No, he can only be the reflection of the Christ – Amen; one must always be able to rely on his truthfulness, his fidelity, his constancy. Paul never had any other ideal; he does not allow the Corinthians to doubt this, for that would be injuring in him the Apostle of Christ, and through him Christ Himself.

> 'We, at least, are not, as many other, adulterating the word of God; but with sincerity, as coming from God, we preach in Christ in God's presence.' *(2, 17)*

Paul identified himself to such a point with his apostolic vocation that for him no problem can be more strictly personal. In him it is always the Apostle who speaks, who writes, who bears witness. The Apostle? that is Christ:

> 'It is now no longer I that live, but Christ lives in me.'
> *(Gal. 2, 20)*

he writes to the Galatians. And the *Letter to the Philippians* delivers over to us the most absolute and definite witness:

> 'For me to live in Christ.' *(Phil. 1, 21)*

C. – *The apostolate, service of the spirit*

From whence does such a sense of his own greatness come to the Apostle? He is a man, after all, and subject to human weaknesses. Can such a boast be justified? Paul answers:

> 'Not that we are sufficient of ourselves to think anything, as from ourselves, but our sufficiency is from God. He also it is Who has made us fit ministers of the new covenant, not of the letter but of the spirit; for the letter kills, but the spirit gives life.' *(3, 5-6)*

In one word, Paul defined the greatness of his ministry: service of the Covenant, and of this eschatological Covenant which the Prophets announced as infinitely superior to the first. The Judaizer – there were some in Corinth and Paul thinks of them here – want to exalt Moses, and to see in Christian revelation only the complement of Mosaic revelation. But the Apostle's mission far surpasses that of Moses himself! As much as the 'Spirit' surpasses the 'letter'!

This absolute antithesis, so admirably formulated that it has become classic, is the finished expression of Paul's thought about the relations between the two Covenants, and hence, definitely, about the real meaning and real greatness of the work of Christ.

Now, we are spontaneously tempted to understand this antithesis as the opposition between the literal interpretation of a text and its interpretation according to inspiration, the 'spirit' which animates it. But here again we are dragged along by our western mentality, which leads us astray far from the real thought of Paul.

This must be understood from a prophecy of Jeremias, which exercised an immense influence on Judaism and on new-born christianity: the Prophecy of the new Covenant.

'Behold, the days shall come, saith the Lord, and I will make a new covenant with the house of Israel and with the house of Juda: Not according to the covenant which I made with their fathers, in the day that I took them by the hand to bring them out of the land of Egypt?... This shall be the covenant that I shall make with the house of Israel (...) I will give my law in their bowels and I will write it in their heart.' (*Jer. 31, 31-33*)

Jeremias opposes there, the two covenants essentially in this: the first expresses itself in a Law exterior to man, in commandments which imposed themselves on him from the outside, written as they were on the tables of stone to which Paul himself alludes on two different occasions:

'You are our letter (of commendation)... clearly you are a letter of Christ, composed by us, written not with ink but with the Spirit of the living God, not on tablets of stone but on fleshly tablets of the heart (...)' *(3, 2-3)*

He writes a little farther on:

'The ministration of death which was engraved in letters upon stones.' *(3, 7)*

As opposed to this first Covenant, the new Covenant which Jeremias proclaims will express itself in a Law interior to man. Obedience will find its source in the depths of souls, in the aspirations of the faithful towards God.
Jeremias did not pronounce the name of 'Spirit'. It was reserved for Ezechiel to do so. His revelation states definitely and completes admirably the Prophecy of Jeremias; it will enlighten us on Paul's thought in this *Letter.*

'I will put a new spirit in their bowels; and I will take away their stony heart out of their flesh and will give them a heart of flesh.' *(Ez. 11, 19)*

So what is this new 'spirit', which will render man sensible to the divine appeals, sensible as 'a heart of flesh' is? It is a profound attitude, an inspiration, an interior dynamism. But what is its source? This is what we shall call it:

'And I will give you a new heart and put a new spirit within you, resumes the Prophet, and I will take away the stony heart out of your flesh and will give you a heart of flesh. And I will put my spirit in the midst of you.' *(Ez. 36, 26-27)*

My spirit! the great revelation is delivered over to us. The New Covenant will be defined by the presence and the action of the Spirit of God. Man can communicate with the divine will, because God will put His Spirit in the midst of him.

Let us not doubt it, Paul, a Jew become Christian, meditated continually on these oracles of the Prophets. Here he recognised, and rightly so, the apogee of the Old Testament and the most brilliant light on the mystery of the New Covenant. It is these oracles which inspire the antithesis, established here, between the Covenant of the letter and the Covenant of the 'Spirit'. Let us not see in this an opposition between 'literal sense' and 'spiritual sense' of the revelation, for this would lead us far from Paul's thought. The 'Spirit' is not here the intention contained in the 'letter'. But it is the very Spirit of God, revealed and given at the eschatological time. Hence the eschatological Covenant is 'Covenant of the Spirit' and the mission of the Apostle 'ministration of the Spirit'. In his *Letter to the Romans,* he will define the Christian life in the same way:

> 'But now we have been set free from the Law, having died to that by which we were held down, so that we may serve in a new spirit and not according to the outworn letter.' *(Rom. 7, 6)*

> 'The letter kills, but the Spirit gives life.' *(3, 6)*

In the light of what we have said about the two Covenants, this contrast is pregnant with its full meaning. The letter is the Mosaic Law, considered in the light of the revelation of Christ and of the Christian faith. The latter make it decayed. This 'Law' kills man, because it has for its effect the multiplication of sin, as Paul will explain at length in his *Letters to the Galatians and to the Romans*

> 'The Law intervened that the offence might abound.' *(Rom. 5, 20)*

> The Law was enacted on account of transgressions.' *(Gal. 3, 19)*

The Mosaic regime, multiplying sin, resulted in the condemnation of man by God, and finally in spiritual death, since, as Paul will write boldly in his *Letter to the Galatians*

> 'For those who rely on the works of the Law are under
> a curse.'   *(Gal. 3, 10)*

Therefore the service of the first Covenant, accomplished by
Moses and all those who followed him, can be legitimately
called 'ministration of death', 'ministration of condemnation' *(3, 7-9)*.
The service of the New Covenant is exactly the opposite;
it is a ministration of life and justice. For it is service of
the Spirit; now the Spirit is a source of life, like the Father
and the Son, because God and God alone, is the real principle of life. We read in the *Gospel according to Saint
John:*

> 'It is the Spirit that gives life; the flesh profits nothing.'
>   *(Jn. 6, 63)*

Saint Peter tells us in his *first Letter* that Christ

> 'Put to death indeed in the flesh, he was brought to life
> in the spirit.'   *(I Pet. 3, 18)*

Moreover, it is very striking that these texts speak to us
about life with respect to the Resurrection: that is explicit
in Peter's *Letter,* and it is the general theme in Saint
John's 'Discourse on the Bread of Life', where we read
mention of the life-giving Spirit. The life of the Spirit is
therefore that of the Resurrection. Christ brought it to men
in the mystery of His own Resurrection and of His heavenly Exaltation. Man receives it in Baptism, when he is born
again of 'water and of the Spirit' *(Jn. 3, 5)*. The letter,
that is the Law, led to death, as the Cross of Christ showed,
coming at the end of the Mosaic regime. The Spirit reveals
a new Covenant, giving to man the life of the Resurrection.

D. – *The apostolate, service of the real glory*

Paul has just opposed the Mosaic Covenant to the christian Covenant. He tells us that the first is the Covenant of the letter, Covenant of death and of condemnation, while the second, which he uses by right of being an Apostle, is Covenant of the Spirit, Covenant of life and of Justice. The greatness of the Apostle's mission appears therefore infinitely superior to that of Moses himself.

Yet! What glory surrounds the first Covenant!

> 'Now if the ministration of death, which was engraved in letters upon stones, was inaugurated in such glory that the children of Israel could not look steadfastly upon the face of Moses on account of the transient glory that shone upon it, shall not the ministration of the spirit be still more glorious? For if there is glory in the ministration that condemned, much more does the ministration that justifies abound in glory. For though the former ministration was glorified, yet in this regard it is without glory, because of the surpassing glory of the latter. For if that which was transient was glorious, much more is that glorious which abides.' *(3, 7-11)*

The glory which was radiating from the face of Moses after his meeting with God on Mount Sinai appears to Paul as the symbol of all the greatness of the Old Covenant. It bore within itself a reflection of the very glory of God.

Therefore if the First Covenant was so glorious, what must have been the brilliance of the New Covenant, which we know to be infinitely superior to the preceding! How great must be the glory promised to the Apostles in virtue of their ministration, if Moses had already been surrounded by a reflection of the very light of God! If a transitory religious regime, resulting in man's condemnation, was so brilliant, what must be the brilliance reserved by God for the new eternal Covenant, which is for all men a permanent source of life and justice!

122

'Having therefore such hope we show great boldness. We do not act as Moses did, who used to put a veil over his face, that the Israelites might not observe the glory of his countenance, which has to pass away... But their minds were darkened; for to this day, when the Old Testament is read to them, the selfsame veil remains, not being lifted to disclose the Christ in whom it is made void. Yes, down to this very day, when Moses is read, the veil covers their hearts; but when they turn in repentance to God, the veil shall be taken away.' *(3, 12-16)*

Paul refers here again to the book of Exodus (34, 33-35). We read there that Moses covered his face with a veil whenever he had finished transmitting to the people the oracles of God. The Bible does not give us the exact reason of this ritual gesture. Hence Paul introduces here a personal explanation, after the manner of the Jewish theologians of this time who had been his teachers.

Here is the explanation: Moses used to put on this veil to prevent the Israelites seeing the brilliance of his face grow dimmer and dimmer until it disappeared. The discovery of this explanation is for Paul, the starting-point of a magnificent allegory, both expressive and original, for it has no parallel in either contemporary Christian or Jewish literature.

Moses' veil was destined to prevent the Israelites from becoming aware of the deficiency of the Covenant of Sinai. The presence of God, the Glory of God which they thought they possessed was but a pale, inconsistent, unefficacious, unreal glimmer of It. According to contemporary philosophy, the only reality was eternity; passing things were but a figure, a shadow. Their Covenant, their Law, the religious regime instituted by Moses, was therefore but a weak and passing image. They made the mistake of relying on this as on an eternal, therefore a solid and real value. The Israelites lived in illusion, in proportion as they regarded as valuable what was only apparently so.

It is understandable, that if Paul devaluates the Covenant of Sinai like this, it is because he judges it, not in the time of Moses, but in his own time, after the manifestation of Christ. For he immediately applies his allegory to the Jewish world of his time. These Jews attached to their Covenant and to their Law are living in illusion. Paul knows them well, he was one of them. They are spiritually blind, as God announced by the Prophet Isaias, because the true reality escapes them. The veil of Moses subsists always; formerly placed on his face, it is placed now for the Jews on the book of Moses, the Law, whose real sense they do not understand. Or, so to speak, this veil is placed on their mind – their 'heart' as Paul says, after the Jewish manner – closing their mind to the real teaching of their Law.

What is this teaching, therefore? What is this true meaning that the Jews, so ardently scrutinising their own Scriptures, can never grasp? It is simply this: that this Law and this Covenant disappear at the coming of Christ. Paul has intentionally used the same word in connection with the Covenant: disappear, that he used in connection with the face of Moses, which also 'used to disappear'. Hence the passing glory of Moses was indeed the symbol of the Old Covenant and of its destiny. As the Hebrews of the time of Moses, when they were listening to him, did not realise that the brilliance which surrounded him was going to disappear in a moment, so too the Jews of today, when they hear Moses again in their synagogues, do not understand that the Covenant of Sinai has reached its end, that 'Christ is the end of the Law' as saint Paul will write to the Romans *(Rom. 10, 4)*.

But, in fact, how could the Jews understand it? It is indeed true that the Law announces its own abolition; but on condition of reading it from a Christian point of view. Paul himself was not converted to Christ by reading the Law; it is after his conversion that he understood that the Law must lead to Christ. It cannot be otherwise for anyone else. Hence Paul continues the allegory of the veil, to show us how the Jew can attain to the real knowledge of the Law. 'But when they turn in repentance to God, the veil shall be taken away *(3, 16)*.

124

We read, in fact, in the *Book of Exodus:*

'Each time that Moses went into the Lord and spoke with Him, he took it away until he came forth.'

(Ex. 34, 34)

In those words, Paul recognised a very beautiful image of the conversion to the Christian faith of a believing Jew, such as he himself was. The veil of Moses symbolising the blindness of the Jew, the entrance of Moses into the Tabernacle where he sees God face to face, become then the symbol of conversion to Christ; because the name of the Lord God is very probably applied here to Jesus, according to the custom of the first Christian Churches. The removal of the veil signifies that the convert gains access to the full knowledge of the Design of God, of the mystery of the two Covenants, one regulated by the other and fulfilling itself only on condition of disappearing. Finally the expression 'each time that', which in the Book of Exodus referred to the successive entries of Moses into the Tabernacle, means here the many individual conversions.

Paul understood well that conversion to Christ must not be expected directly from a knowledge of Scripture; it is on the contrary, recognition of the fact of Christ which sheds full light on the whole of revelation. Such was, besides, the thought of the Primitive Church, as the Discourses of Peter and of the Apostles that we read in the *Acts* testify. With this light of Christ, real liberty is given to man. Because blindness is a slavery, the veil on the face is the image of a constraint, a real captivity, which is opposed to the full confidence of the Christian attitude. But what is this slavery if not that of the Law, of which Paul will speak at length, in his *Letters to the Galatians* and to the *Romans*? Is it not the slavery of these ordinances, exterior to man, of 'this letter which kills' because it provokes sin, which leads to death? And what is the liberty of the Christian but the liberty of the Spirit? The Spirit is liberty itself; like the wind it blows where it wills *(Jn. 3, 8)*. Thus man who is reborn of the Spirit finds himself delivered from all the servitudes of the Law, of the flesh, of sin.

125

'Now the Lord is the Spirit; and where the Spirit of the Lord is there is freedom.'   *(3, 17)*

It is impossible to affirm more strongly that the work of Christ is completely summed up in the gift of the Spirit. He alone shows men where true liberty is to be found.

The allegory of the veil makes us pass progressively from the situation of Moses and of the Jews to the situation of the Christian. Paul now defines this:

'But we all with faces unveiled, reflecting as in a mirror the glory of the Lord, are being transformed into His very image, from glory to glory, as through the Spirit of the Lord.'   *(3, 18)*

In the New Covenant, therefore, each Christian has become a new Moses. Still Moses had his face covered only on rare occasions, and the glory which he radiated disappeared rapidly; the Christian, on the contrary, stands always in the presence of the Lord, in immediate contact with His glory, and this glory which he possesses, being the reality of the Divinity Itself, can neither grow dim nor disappear. Is Paul thinking here of mystic contemplation? Certainly not, because what he says includes all Christians; now, all are not called to contemplation. Would it be a question of 'vision', in Saint John's sense of the word, vision through faith and grace? Yes, undoubtedly, because faith and grace bring us into communion with Christ. But, more concretely still, Paul probably evokes Baptism here; this inserts us really in Christ. Let us not forget that in the Church where Paul lived, baptism was already called 'illumination' as the *Letter to the Hebrews* will testify *(6, 4; 10, 32)*.

Hence, Paul defines the Christian as the person who, after the example of Moses in the Tabernacle is in uninterrupted communion with God. He is intimately penetrated with the radiation of the Glory of Christ. Of course, we cannot interpret the brilliance of which Saint Paul speaks in the exterior visible sense of the word. Thus, the same word, Glory, which when applied to Moses meant the visible radiation of the divinity, means, when applied to the Christian, the intimate transfiguration of his being by baptismal regeneration.

The Christian is infinitely greater than Moses. Not alone does he not cover his face in the presence of God; neither does he cover it in the presence of men. He always bears witness to his permanent communion with God. He radiates, mysteriously but efficaciously, the glory really present in him from his Baptism. Such is the greatness of man in the New Covenant; a new greatness never before revealed of the situation of man face to face with God and his fellow-men.

That is not all: This greatness is continually increasing. 'We are being transformed into his very image, *from glory to glory*' as the words in the text tell us. The present of the Greek verb is essentially continuous: we are being transformed... and the expression 'from glory to glory' is a Jewish one which expresses the progressive acquisition of a perfection or of a totality, as we see in this verse of the psalm: 'they will go from strength to strength' i.e. with an ever-increasing strength *(Ps. 84, 8)*.

Consequently, the Christian is not only the person who communicates in the glory of Christ and reflects it; in Him, this communion is always growing deeper and more intense. He is progressively divinised by his union with the Lord. Divinisation which is, throughout his earthly existence, the very blossoming of his baptismal illumination. From this birth 'of the water and of the Spirit' *(Jn. 3, 5)*, the action of the Spirit of the Lord is continually renewing man until the day when it will make him perfectly transparent to the Glory of the Lord in the resurrection.

We have already seen that the problem in this *Letter* is that of the apostolate of Paul, and on that very account, that of the authentic apostolate. This problem led Paul to oppose the two Covenants, in order to highlight the infinite superiority of the Christian apostolate. But, quite naturally, the theme of the New Covenant led us to define the situation and the greatness of all Christians.

Paul returns now to the Apostle's own situation. He will apply to it what he has discovered of the Christian in general: the Apostle will be defined also with reference to the Glory of the Lord.

> 'Discharging therefore this ministry in accordance with the mercy shown us, we do not lose heart. (...) but making known the truth, we commend ourselves to every man's conscience in the sight of God. And if our Gospel also, is veiled, it is veiled only to those who are perishing. In their case the god of this world has blinded their unbelieving minds, that they should not see the light of the Gospel of the glory of Christ, Who is the image of God. For we preach not ourselves but Jesus Christ as Lord, and ourselves merely as your servants in Jesus.'
>
> *(4, 1-5)*

The Apostle therefore places himself in the Design of God, between Christ and men. He is turned towards Christ, unique object of his message and unique raison d'être of his action and of his behaviour. He is turned towards man to be their servant, as Paul had already proclaimed in the *First Letter* at that same Church of Corinth:

> 'Free though I was to all, unto all I have made myself a slave.'   *(I Cor. 9, 19)*

But, of course, he is turned towards man only in view of Christ. He is the servant of his brothers only because he is first and foremost servant of Christ! The mission of the Apostle, and his greatness with respect to Moses, can only be understood if we set out from Christ.

Now Christ Himself defined Himself 'the image of God'. What Moses was only imperfectly and in an ephemeral manner, what the christian is by participation, that Christ is, properly and fully. He is image of the invisible God *(Col. 1, 15)* and 'brightness of His glory', as the *Letter to the Hebrews* will tell us. Let us understand thoroughly that the word image in the New Testament, calls up not a mere resemblance, more or less exterior, but the whole reality. Image of God, Christ possesses the Glory of His Father and manifests it to us. Apostolic preaching, in its turn, strives to reveal this glorious Christ to us. The Gospel is but the proclamation of a glory, the Glory of Christ! As the whole of the Old Testament was the revelation of the Glory of God, so the Gospel is the revelation of the glory of Christ. The function of the Apostles, surpasses and prolongs that of Moses and the Prophets. The whole of revelation, in its two Covenants, becomes a manifestation of Glory: at first an imperfect manifestation in Moses, i.e. in the regime of the Law; and, at the end of time, a manifestation in the fullness of Christ,

'We saw His glory, glory as of the only-begotten of the Father,'   *(Jn. 1, 14)*

Saint John will write.

The synthesis of all this Pauline theology of Glory is given to us in a very beautiful conclusion:

'For God, Who commanded light to shine out of darkness, has shone in our hearts, to give enlightenment concerning the knowledge of the glory of God, shining on the face of Jesus Christ.'   *(4, 6)*

The work of God is wholly a work of light. Throughout history God does not cease to illuminate men. On the very first day he made His light shine in the midst of darkness; thus began for us the revelation of His glory. Today he reveals this same glory in the souls of those to whom He makes Himself known: Paul is evidently thinking here of His own conversion.
But if God thus chooses to reveal Himself to certain men, it is not for themselves alone. The manifestation of His real glory must reach all men, for He is the creator and

Lord of all. God, when He reveals Himself to His elect, assigns them their task: to spread the knowledge of His glory. To make the presence, the efficacy, the reality of God shine before the eyes of men; such is the ultimate definition of the apostolate.

We know that it signifies nothing else but the preaching of Christ. For, in a perfect manner, from the face of Christ radiates this glory of which Moses used to receive a reflection, and whose brilliance transfigures, us, Christians.

'He who sees me sees also the Father,' *(Jn. 14, 9)* says Jesus Himself.

E. – *The apostolate, death and life*

The fundamental law of Christian existence is that of life and death. But Paul discovers its most total application in the apostolic existence, which appears throughout this Letter as the apogee, or preferably, the very type of Christian existence.

Paul realised better than anyone else, what a striking contrast exists between the greatness of the apostolic mission and the weakness of man to whom it is confided:

> 'But we carry this treasure in vessels of clay to show
> that the abundance of the power is God's and not ours.'
> *(4, 7)*

The whole theme of strength and weakness is gathered in this one sentence. This theme which constitutes one of the essential expressions of Pauline mysticism he will develop at length in his apologia at the end of this *Letter*.

But the paradox is developed and deepened:

> 'In all things we suffer tribulation; but are not distressed. We are straitened; but are not destitute.
> We suffer persecution; but are not forsaken. We are cast down; but we perish not.
> Always bearing about in our body the mortification of

Jesus, that the life also of Jesus may be made manifest in our bodies.

For we who live are always delivered unto death for Jesus' sake, that the life also of Jesus may be made manifest in our mortal flesh.

So then death worketh in us; but life in you.'

(4, 8-12)

So Paul discovers in his apostolic experience a paradox which really poses him a question: he is in constant danger of death – the serious trial undergone in Asia was another sign of this – however he succeeds in overcoming so many obstacles and dangers. What is the profound meaning of this double continual experience, of death and life, of defeat and victory?

The answer to this question, Paul finds in Christ. For in the mystery of Christ the same paradox is revealed: weakness and strength, death and life. It appears first in a general manner, in the whole earthly life of Christ. It is marked by persecution, failure and humiliation; however throughout this same life the continual unfolding of the power of God is very evident. But, above all, the apostolic paradox is realised in the mystery of the death and resurrection of Christ, because as Paul himself will say at the end of this *Letter*:

'For though He was crucified through weakness, yet He lives through the power of God.'   (13, 4)

Paul opposing his apostolic experience to the mystery of Christ understands that his trials, his difficulties, this ever-threatening death are only the dying of Christ, continued in his witnesses; while the strength which the apostle possesses in spite of all, the incomprehensible resistance which he opposes to the powers of destruction, are the manifestation in him of the life of the glorious Christ and an anticipation, in this present life, of the glory of the Resurrection.

The law of the Apostle's life is therefore to pass through

the states of Christ. It is only in this communion that it gets its true meaning and finds the source of its power. The general law of Christian existence applies fully to apostolic existence; for the former consists in living one's baptism, which is insertion in the dead and risen Christ. Like the Christian, the apostle live these two states of Christ constantly and simultaneously. Because it is in the midst of trials that the definite triumph of life is really inaugurated.

Paul will express this faith in the triumph of life in the celebrated antithesis of the outer man and the inner man:

> 'We do not lose heart... Even though our outer man is decaying, yet our inner man is being renewed day by day.'
> (4, 16)

The inner man? Another passage from the Epistles explains this expression, puzzling enough at first:

> 'That the Father may grant you from His glorious riches, to be strengthened with power through His Spirit unto the progress of the inner man.'
> (Eph. 3, 16)

The inner man is not the soul, or the mind as opposed to the body; it is the whole being, renewed by baptism, 'reborn' of the Holy Spirit. Paul calls it elsewhere 'the new man', a clearer expression, because it stresses the belonging of the regenerated being to the new creation, the eschatological creation.

From this time the outer man, 'who is decaying', is not only the body taken in isolation, but also feeble humanity which still subsists after baptismal regeneration. It is the human being submitting to all the trials, persecutions, agonies of which Paul has just spoken; our being in which the state of the dying Christ is manifest at every moment. Moreover, there is no direct allusion to sin or to concupisence, to the weakness inherent in our human nature, until the dawn of the glorious resurrection. We are the outer man, we still belong to this perishable creation. We are destined to be transformed with it, after the passage through the great trial of death. Already we have a presentiment of it in our weaknesses and in our sufferings. Even after baptism, the life that we live remains marked by death, due to sin. That is why our outer man 'is decaying', uniting us thus to the mystery of the death of Christ. But, simultaneously, a superior principle of life is acting in us. Our inner man 'is being renewed from day to day'; the expression indicates clearly enough the continuous character of this renewal. From his baptism, the Christian is engaged in a double process: one of destruction, the other of regeneration. Israel lived these two states, successively; but, since the Resurrection of Christ till the last coming, the Christian is living them simultaneously. This double process will end in the total triumph of the inner man. No part of us is called to perish. But our whole being must be transformed by the principle of new life, the Spirit, until we finally blaze forth in glory.

In the case of the Apostle, this double process of death and of life, assumes a still higher value. God has delivered over His Son to death in order to give us life; so too he delivers over his envoys, more than all others, to sufferings and persecutions in order that life may radiate from them.

'Unless the grain of wheat falls into the ground and dies, it remains alone; But if it dies it brings forth much fruit,' (Jn. 12, 24)
Jesus used to say.

Paul echoes his Master's words when he resumes in one word his whole experience as an apostle living the christian paradox to the full.

'Thus death is at work in us but life in you.' (4, 12)

All that Paul understands because he lives in faith.

'But since we have the same spirit of faith, as shown in

133

that which is written – 'I believed and so I spoke,' – we also believed, wherefore we also speak. For we know that he who raised up Jesus will raise up us also with Jesus, and will place us with you. (...) We look not at the things that are seen, but at the things that are not seen. For the things that are seen are temporal, but the things that are not seen are eternal.'   *(4, 13-18)*

The believer, the apostle is living in a new light from the time of his illumination by baptismal grace; he is awaiting that grace that will launch him into the brilliant light of the Resurrection.

'Thus it says:
Awake, sleeper,
Arise from among the dead
And Christ will enlighten thee.'   *(Eph. 5, 14)*

This light of Christ reveals to the believer the world of invisible realities, i.e. inaccessible not only to the senses but also to the reason of man. In the story of the prophet Eliseus we read an example of this. It is both picturesque and rich in the theological sense:

'The servant of Eliseus saw an army round about the city, and horses and chariots. And he told him saying: Alas, alas my lord, what shall we do? But he answered: Fear not; for there are more with us than with them. And Eliseus prayed and said: 'Lord, open his eyes, that he may see. And the Lord opened the eyes of the servant, and he saw. And behold, the mountain was full of horses, and chariots of fire round about Eliseus.'
                    (4 Kg. 6, 15-17).

The total faith of Eliseus in the power of God was really a 'vision of the invisible', as the *Letter to the Hebrews* puts it with regard to Moses *(Heb. 11, 27)*. The servant had to see to believe, but Eliseus firmly believed without having to see a sign or a prodigy; he was living in constant communion with the active presence of God.

So too with the Christian. He is always in communion with a world unsuspected by the carnal man. Not an ideal world, such as philosophers forge, but the very concrete world of eschatological realities, of the supreme eschatological reality: Resurrection, glory, exaltation with Christ at the right hand of God.

Even so, the believer does not escape from the present world. On the contrary, the eye of faith recognises the presence of the eschatological world in our universe and in our life; it discovers that the present world is penetrated with this mystery of the resurrection and of glory which is already at work there. Hence faith is not an ideal vision of the world but a realistic vision, which assumes all present realities, including the weakness of 'our mortal flesh', in the transforming light of the Spirit. Apostolic experience, and through it Christian experience, as just defined by Paul, are unintelligible unless regarded from the viewpoint of faith.

F. – *The Christian in the presence of the mystery of death*

Paul has just concluded his development on apostolic experience by the sparkling affirmation of the eye of faith, the only authentic vision of the world for the apostle, for the Christian. This eye of faith unveils the invisible world of eschatological realities, for which his baptism destines him. Hence, quite naturally, Paul pauses a while on this mystery of the Christian's destiny.

> 'For we know that if this tent, the earthly house in which we dwell be destroyed, we have a building from God, a house not made by human hands, eternal in the heavens.'   *(5, 1)*

Paul does not claim to teach us anything new and personal here. 'We know', he writes, which shows clearly that he is appealing to the doctrine of faith known to the Christians of Corinth.

But he expresses this doctrine in an original form. Our eschatological destiny, is for him the passage from one building to another, from an earthly house to a heavenly one. What does he mean? What is this earthly building and this heavenly building?

We do not find much in the Bible to explain this image to us. However, the Book of Job speaks to us about

'they that dwell in houses of clay who have an earthly foundation.'
(*Job 4, 19*)

These dwellers are men; the house of clay is our body, by allusion to the story of Creation in Genesis 2.

Similarly we see in the 'Canticle of Ezechias' that the building is an image of the body, from which man is separated at the hour of death:

'My building is at an end and it is rolled away from me as a shepherd's tent.'
(*Is. 38, 12*)

These two texts put us on the right road for understanding Paul. But Hellenistic literature is much more enlightening still. It attests for us in a certain manner, that the image of the building and the very term tent had become classic for describing the body, temporary residence of the soul. The use of this image was moreover connected with the great philosophic problem of the Greeks: the relations of the soul and the body, a problem which did not at all worry Israelite philosophers.

We find exactly this same image in a book of the Old Testament which was strongly influenced by Hellenism, the *Book of Wisdom*.

'For the corruptible body is a load upon the soul, and the earthly tent presseth down the mind which museth upon many thoughts.'
(*Wis. 9, 15*)

Even in the New Testament, the Second Letter of Saint Peter gives us a text very near that of our *Letter to the Corinthians:*

'As long as I am in this tent, I think it right to arouse you by a reminder, knowing as I do that the putting off of my tent is at hand, just as our Lord Jesus Christ signified to me.'
(*II Pet. 1, 13-14*)

The earthly building, the tent of which Saint Paul speaks to us, is therefore our body, our present body, with all its weaknesses, its deficiencies, its infirmities, showing early signs of the destruction to which it is condemned. Paul noticed these foreboding signs of his departure, during the serious illness which he had just undergone in Asia. Undoubtedly he continues to feel them in his flesh; they remind him constantly that this earthly life is only a passage, and this body a 'shepherd's tent' which he must soon leave.

But the believer knows that he leaves it for a heavenly building, an eternal house, not made by the hand of man. In the choice of terms Paul stresses very intentionally the opposition between our provisional earthly habitation and our heavenly habitation, 'building', a solid and definite construction which is the work of God. In a different perspective, the *Letter to the Hebrews* establishes quite a similar contrast: for it speaks to us about Abraham 'dwelling in tents with Isaac and Jacob, the co-heirs of the same promise; for he was looking for the city with fixed foundations, of which city the architect and the builder is God... Therefore God has prepared for them a city' (*Heb. 11, 9-10...16*).

This building towards which we tend, Paul calls it 'house not made by the hands of man'. Here again, the *Letter to the Hebrews* explains the meaning of this to us: not of this creation (*Heb. 9, 11*).

Our future dwelling does not belong to the order of realities that we know: carnal and perishable, but to a superior order, that of spiritual and everlasting realities: Our glorious body will be like our present body, the creation of God; but it will be entirely penetrated with the Spirit of God and freed from all heaviness of flesh and blood.

If Paul speaks of this heavenly body in the present: 'we have in heaven' it is not at all that he imagined our glorious body as actually existing in heaven where it would be quite prepared by God. The present: 'we have' evokes here the absolute certainty of faith, and the consciousness that baptism gives us, already, as well as the presence of the Holy Spirit, the pledge of a glorious resurrection. Won't Paul write to the Ephesians:

'God has brought us to life together with Christ, and raised us up together, and seated us together in heaven in Christ Jesus.' *(Eph. 2, 6)*

But now Paul reveals to us an inner grief, a painful tension, which is the lot of every christian living his Christianity profoundly:

'For in this present state we groan, desiring to be clothed over with our habitation that is from heaven;
Yet, so that we be found clothed, not naked.
For we who are in this tent sigh under our burden, because we do not wish to be unclothed, but rather clothed over, that what is mortal may be swallowed up by life.'
(5, 2-4)

Inner tension of the Christian... We know indeed that we are called to another condition than our present state: a glorious condition where we shall fully apprehend ourselves. Nothing is more desirable than this new state. The Christian really conscious of his baptism, like Paul, aspires ardently to this transformation, this 'redemption of the body' as the *Letter to the Romans* calls it. But at the same time he cannot help enduring a real agony when faced with the necessary trial: the passage through death, according to the image of the seed evoked by Paul himself in his *first Letter to the Corinthians (15, 36)*. Death, this stripping off of our body, presented here, in a new image also very hellenistic, as the casting off of a garment, has for us an abnormal violent, mysterious character, which fills us with trouble and agony.

For a Paul, it is not a matter of regret for the loss of life, of sunlight, of the joys of youth, as was the case with the tragic Greeks, or in the biblical books of *Job* and of *Ecclesiastes*, in the 'Canticle of Ezechias'... Still less is it a matter of the uncertainty or doubt which follows death; because no one has expressed more strongly than Paul, and on this very page, his certainty of union with Christ. But Paul here is a typical Jew, who gives all its value to the body, while never really developing the distinction still less the opposition soul-body. In spite of the Greek images of 'house', of 'garment' of the soul, Paul here expresses a metaphysical agony, fully inscribed in the Jewish line of thought: the trouble which lays hold on man at the thought of this uprooting of a part of himself, of part of his personality, of his being a man.

Would there be any means of avoiding this painful separation, any way to Glory without passing through death? Yes, according to the same teaching of Paul there is another way. Did he not write to the Thessalonians:

'The dead in Christ will rise up first. Then we who live, who survive shall be caught up together with them.'
(*I Th. 4, 16-17*)

And also this, in his first *Letter to the Corinthians*:

'We shall all indeed rise, but we shall not all be changed.' (*I Cor. 15, 51*)

A certain number of mankind will be still alive at the coming of Christ: those will not have to pass through the trial of death, to 'strip themselves' as Saint Paul says, of their present body. They will be transformed, spiritualised, putting on the glorious body as it were, over the other, in this sense that there will be no uprooting, no intimate separation from themselves, but absorption of all that is mortal and corruptible by the all-powerful forces of life. This Paul already expressed perfectly in his preceding *Letter*

> 'For this corruptible body must put on incorruption, and this mortal body must put on immortality. But when this mortal body puts on immortality, then shall come to pass the word that is written, 'Death is swallowed up in victory'.'   *(I Cor. 15, 53-54)*

Agony in the presence of death, so noticeable in Greek as well as in biblical thought, found its Christian expression in this page of Paul. The believer knows that glory is promised to him; already, he possesses its first fruits; he is sure of entering fully into it some day. But man hesitates and draws back from this painful passage which gives access to it; he would like to escape from this trial the very thought of which is unbearable to him.

But this inner drama is solved at last by abandonment to God, the Author of our destiny, Who gave us, by the presence of the Spirit, the certainty that He will fulfil His promise:

> 'Now He Who made us for this destiny is God, Who has given us the Spirit as its pledge.'   *(5, 5)*

Hence at the end of it all, what will be the practical attitude of the believer in the presence of the mystery of death?

It will be, first of all, an unshakeable courage, Paul insists on this fundamental disposition:

> 'Always full of courage then (...) Yes, we are full of courage.'   *(5, 6-8)*

Courage is here the rejection of trouble and hesitation before such a terrifying prospect; it is this instinctive refusal that Paul himself expressed so dramatically a moment

140

before. The term that Paul uses here belonged to the language of contemporary moral philosophy. We read in the *Phedon*: 'No one has a justified courage, a reasonable courage in the presence of death, unless he is able to prove that the soul is totally immortal and imperishable'.

The Stoics loved to define as a 'full courage' the ideal of calmness and of firmness which was theirs when face to face with trials, sickness, and especially death. Paul uses this term to express the peace and the certainty which the Christian shows facing the most agonising of mysteries.

What is the foundation of this courage of the believer? Knowledge of the faith:

> 'Therefore having always confidence, knowing that while we are in the body we are absent from the Lord.'
> *(5, 6)*

The certainty of the believer is not founded on philosophic analysis but on revelation. It is not, primarily, a certainty of the immortality of the soul, but rather a certainty of the glorious existence of a Person, to Whom we are called to unite ourselves definitely by sharing His Glory.

Therefore we have, while living here on this earth, the feeling that we are exiles. 'For me, to die is gain', Paul will write a little later to the Philippians *(1, 21)*. Does it mean handing in one's resignation to the present life, devalorising our existence as men? Not at all! No more than when Paul invited us to cast our eyes on 'invisible realities.' On Paul's lips, it means a keen sense of the baptismal reality. What is this reality? In one word: union with Christ. This union, once begun, tends to its own fulfilment. Of itself it is continually developing, in the depths of our being. Paul wants us to become aware of this development, of this march of time towards its end.

Hence fear and trouble in the presence of death are effaced by a higher consideration: that of the end which it permits us to attain:

> 'We prefer to be exiled from the body and to be at home with the Lord.'
> *(5, 8)*

The *Letter to the Philippians* will echo this:

'I desire to depart and to be with Christ.' *(Phil. 1, 23)*

Is this Paul's last word, the supreme witness of the knowledge of a believer and of an Apostle? No.
There remains a last purification of the desire and of the will:

'And therefore, we strive, whether in the body or out of it, to be pleasing to the Lord.'
(5, 9)

Thus, in the end, the highest Pauline mysticism always brings us back to the concrete reality of our daily existence. Agony in the presence of death is solved in the desire for union with Christ; the desire for union results in the will to obey the Lord – today.

G. – *Ambassador of Christ*

The will to obey. What does that mean for the apostle, if not to make every effort to conquer the world for Jesus Christ? For the flame of this love burns in the heart of the apostle:

'The love of Christ impels us.'
(5, 14)

and even if he would like to hide from it he cannot, no more than Jeremias could formerly:

'There came in my heart as a burning fire set up on my bones; and I was wearied not being able to bear it.'
(Jer. 20, 9)

One single thought dominates the life of the apostle, and, in truth obsesses him; this thought is the supreme act of faith which transforms the whole of existence:

'One died for all, therefore all died. Christ died for all, in order that they who are alive may live no longer for themselves, but for him Who died for them and rose again.' *(5, 14-15)*

In these few words, Paul has collected the whole Christian *Credo*; all its faith, all its morality. His *Letters* which abound in striking formulas, present none more striking than that. 'All died', because we are but one in Christ the new Adam; head of the whole human race he resumes it all in himself. Christ is indeed the Son of Man, Man par excellence, Who is to appear at the end of time but is none the less first in the Design of God. Yes, in Him all died: died to sin, to the Law, to flesh and blood, which were holding us captive. Christ broke by His death and resurrection the yoke which was pressing on us. He liberated us. But since that time we belong to Him: the slave becomes the property of the person who redeems him. Thus Israel redeemed from Egypt in the first ages of salvation became the slave of God Who said,

'For the children of Israel are my servants whom I brought forth out of the land of Egypt.' *(Lev. 25, 55)*

Today the baptised person becomes a servant of Christ. He no longer belongs to himself. He cannot dispose egoistically of a life which was paid for by the Sacrifice of Christ. Let not the Corinthians be surprised therefore at certain attitudes of Paul, at his behaviour sometimes flying into a passion, sometimes prudently moderate. In all this he has not his personal interests in view but solely those of Christ and of the Corinthians themselves. Don't judge him then 'according to the flesh', in a purely human and exterior manner. Because he Paul, feels for certain that his life has been transformed by faith, and that his vision of the world and of men has been transfigured:

'Henceforth we know no one according to the flesh.' *(5, 16)*

We must not then expect Paul to let himself be stopped by human considerations; opinion of one person or another, success or failure, contradictions and oppositions. He feels that he has gone beyond all that, and wants to be understood. It is not that he denies all feeling, all affection; he has so often expressed his attachment, his tenderness even. But he knows that the human feelings of the believer, of the apostle must be transfigured by reference to Christ. Moreover,

> 'And even though we have known Christ according to the flesh, yet now we know him so no longer.' *(5, 16)*

Our knowledge of Christ Himself must not be 'carnal'. The Gospels, especially Saint John's, state clearly that the Apostles really knew Christ only after the Resurrection and Pentecost. Until then, of course, they recognised in Him the Envoy of God, the Prophet, the Messiah; but, all the same, they judged Him very humanly, they almost shared the reactions of their milieu in the presence of the miracles, the requirements, the trials of their Master. The Resurrection and Pentecost transformed them. Until then, they knew Jesus of Nazareth; from that on they entered into the mystery of Christ. Until then, He was the Master, they were the disciples; from that on He is the Lord, and they His witnesses. Until then, He appeared to them aureoled with human glory; from that on, he reveals to them the glory of God.

We must all follow the same road. Our faith must be able to rise above the accidental aspects of the life of Christ, to which we are often tempted to attach ourselves childishly, in order to attach itself totally to the mystery of the Cross and Resurrection. Or rather, our faith must be deep enough, and supernatural enough to understand that nothing is accidental in the life of the Lord; everything there concerns the mystery of salvation, everything there refers to the Cross and Resurrection. As there is nothing superfluous or purely anecdotal in the Bible, everything in it, down to the smallest detail being ordered by the knowledge of God, so there is nothing superfluous or indifferent in the life of the Lord; everything there is ordered by redemption and glory. Such is the viewpoint from which we must read and meditate on the Gospel; then we shall know Christ as Paul wanted us to know Him.

Ambassador of Christ! Paul wants no other title, because he has no other reason for living. He asks of his Christians an act of faith in his mission. Certainly this act of faith is not always easy: the envoy of Christ remains a man, with his weaknesses and his mistakes, his faults of temperament and character. All the same some visible signs come to authenticate his mission. At the end of his *Letter*, Paul will invoke miracles and prodigies wrought among the Corinthians with this end in view *(12, 12)*. But, nowadays, we are more sensible of other signs which Paul enumerates here, in a page whose sincerity, emotion, passion are a master-piece of eloquence:

'Let us conduct ourselves in all circumstances as God's ministers, in much patience; in tribulations, in hardships, in distresses; in stripes, in imprisonments, in tumults; in labours, in sleepless nights, in fastings; in innocence, in knowledge, in long-sufferings; in kindness, in the Holy Spirit, in unaffected love; in the word of truth, in the power of God; with the armour of justice on the right hand and on the left; in honor and dishonor, in evil report and good report; as deceivers and yet truthful, as unknown and yet well known, as dying and behold, we live, as chastised but not killed, as sorrowful yet always rejoicing, as poor yet enriching many, as having nothing yet possessing all things.'   *(6, 4-10)*

H. – *Call to generosity*

In the communities of the Greek world, Paul organised a collection for the Church of Jerusalem. For the latter possessed scarcely any personal resources and had a heavy burden: the maintenance of the poor, mentioned as early as this time, in the Acts. For the Churches of Greece to give help to the Church of Jerusalem was a gesture of christian fraternity and gratitude; it was even more than that, a real symbol of unity in Christ. Corinth, by reason of its importance should participate in this collection. So Paul invites the Corinthians to do so, but not without a hint of malicious irony:

> 'Now as you abound in everything – in faith, in utterance, in knowledge, in all zeal, and in your love for us – may you excel in this gracious work also.' (8, 7)

The Corinthians must have been stung to the quick..., but Paul has another argument to bring forward in favour of this mutual aid:

> 'For you know the graciousness of our Lord Jesus Christ – how, being rich, He became poor for your sakes, that by His poverty you might become rich.'
>
> (8, 9)

Nobody knows as well as Paul how to raise a debate, to treat a question on the highest plane, to shed light on a problem by a superior consideration. And this, without pretension and without artifice, but in the most natural and spontaneous manner, typical of a really great mind. The most ordinary commonplace question – a collection – assumes suddenly a profound meaning and a greatness to which no one can remain insensible.

> 'I do not speak as commanding (...). In this matter I am giving advice.'

Have Christians to be commanded when charity is at stake? It is enough to 'depict before their eyes Jesus Christ crucified' to use another expression of Saint Paul (*Gal. 3, 1*). After that, it ought not to be necessary to command.

Christ gives His own the supreme example of generosity: that which does not express what one has but what one is. 'Rich' in all the splendour of the divine nature, he became 'poor' with all the weaknesses of our human nature, and a human nature voluntarily humble and despised. He became poor in His life, in the sufferings of His passion, in His death on the Cross. Now, it is for us that He did that. He wanted to make an unheard of exchange with us: to take upon Himself our poverty, and to communicate His riches to us. He became Son of Man, in order that man should become son of God. Paul says admirably: he enriched us by His poverty. A paradoxical affirmation yet so profoundly correct: the Incarnation, 'poverty' of God, is the source of our riches.

We must pause here to evoke what Paul will write to the Philippians a little later:

> 'Have this mind in you which was also in Christ Jesus, Who though He was by nature God did not consider being equal to God a thing to be clung to, but emptied Himself, taking the nature of a slave and being made like unto men. And appearing in the form of man, he humbled Himself, becoming obedient to death, even to death on a cross.'   *(Phil. 2, 5-9)*

Why do such texts awaken echoes in our hearts? Is it only because they bring us proof that the faith of the first Christians in the divinity of Christ, in the Incarnation, and Redemption, was identical with ours? It is, much more still, because they give testimony that these truths of faith were intimately connected with daily life. In a matter of charity, mutual understanding, mutual help, spontaneously the Christian conscience turned towards Christ. In meditation on His mysteries, it found light and strength, those very things which we need today and which we must learn to draw from the same source.

I. – *The great apologia of Paul*

The pages which come now, the last of this *Letter*, constitute an apologia of Paul by himself. With a vivaciousness, a strength, an almost unparalleled eloquence, he answers the attacks launched against his person and his mission. Not that Paul thought it necessary to defend his poor human person; but through him, in him, the Apostle of Christ was attacked. His answer is the greatest testimony that he gave us of his apostolic experience.

Paul announces his next visit to the Church of Corinth; a visit which is likely to be stern. It is not however that Paul likes to be either stern or violent, like certain so-called apostles with a fairly large following in Corinth:

> 'For you suffer if a man enslaves you, if a man devours you, if a man takes from you, if a man is arrogant, if a man slaps your face. I speak to my own shame, as though we had been weak.' *(11, 20-21)*

Paul's refinement in preceding contests – he had so many with this community – was not understood by the Corinthians. They saw in it only weakness, being too unrefined themselves to recognise in it 'the meekness and gentleness of Christ' *(10, 11)*. Paul undoubtedly had an ardent temperament, which sometimes reached the boiling-point of violence; he left us proof enough of this in his *Letters* and n his animated career. But being an Apostle of Christ he understood the lesson of the Beatitudes and that of the Cross. In the war that was his life, he would have wished for the weapons of his warfare, meekness, indulgence and forgiveness. Because it is indeed a war that is waged, but not a war 'according to the flesh' *(10, 3)*, i.e. in the human manner, and with an earthly object in view. At stake in the war he wages in the world and in the Church of Corinth itself, is the Kingdom of God. The enemy he meets everywhere is human wisdom, to which the Corinthians were already so attached. We know this from his preceding *Letter*:

148

'We make war on reasoning and every lofty thing that exalts itself against the knowledge of God, bringing every mind into captivity to the obedience of Christ.'

(10, 4-5)

Indeed, the eschatological times have arrived. Of these the Prophet says:

'Because the day of the Lord of Hosts shall Be upon everyone that is proud and highminded Upon everyone that is arrogant and he shall be humbled.' *(Is. 2, 12)*

On this account does the Apostle's mission consist in condemning, or, according to the expression Paul himself uses in his *First Letter to the Corinthians,* 'make war on' all the thought, the culture, the wisdom of mankind? Not at all, Christianity does not claim to destroy human thought and culture, or to supersede them. Paul's affirmation is much more nuanced: what he wants is to 'bring every mind into captivity' to the obedience of Christ. Conquest, not destruction, is the point under discussion. The military term used here is only an image; evidently it does not signify conquest by military strength or moral pressure, for it never entered Paul's mind to use such means of propaganda. Christian teaching wants to bring about the effective submission of human thought; but this submission is defined as obedience to Christ. Now, there is no other obedience to Christ but that of faith. In his *Letter to the Romans* Paul will tell us that his grace and his apostolic mission are resumed in this: to bring about obedience to the faith among all the nations *(Rom. 1,5; 15,18; 16,26)?* Christian conquest is but the free acceptance, by the mind of man, of this superior value i.e. the knowledge of God and of His Christ:

'You shall know the truth says Jesus and the truth shall make you free.' *(Jn. 8, 32)*

Hence Paul can legitimately proclaim that the arms of his

warfare are not 'carnal'. The authentic envoy of Christ, the Apostle really worthy of this name is a stranger to ruse, manoeuvres, and interested calculations. He embarks on a work of spiritual conquest; he, a man in the midst of men, can do this only with arms endowed with 'divine power'. What are these arms which 'demolish strongholds' *(10, 4)*? Paul has already defined them: constancy in trials, purity, knowledge, longanimity, charity, justice... *(6, 4-7)*. These are the fruits of the Holy Spirit in the soul of his servants. In the main, it is the Spirit Himself Who gives to the Apostle, still 'living in the flesh', the non-carnal arms of the warfare of God.

Paul has just defined the attitude and action of the authentic apostle. He defended himself against the criticism levelled at him in Corinth. He proceeds now to the attack. They provoked him; he takes up the challenge. Facing all his adversaries, he will boast in his turn:

> 'What I am saying I am not speaking according to the Lord, but as it were in foolishness. Since many boast according to the flesh, I too will boast.'
>
> *(11, 17-18)*

Paul will therefore place himself on the same ground as his enemies. That is why he speaks of 'foolishness'. His foolishness consists in accepting the proposed discussion; instead of orientating the debate towards the superior principles of justice, charity, humility, he accepts the proposed subject, adopts reactions, attitudes, judgments similar to those of his adversaries; in a word he abandons – for a moment – the Wisdom of God, to speak and reason according to the wisdom of man, according to flesh and blood since, after all, these are the attitudes that the Corinthians who think themselves so wise – accept most gladly.

Of course, Paul says all this with a biting and even cruel irony:

'For you gladly put up with fools, because you are wise
yourselves,'   (11, 19)

which leads us to think that the Corinthians were very
sensitive. Paul had understood that the time had come to
give a lesson: he had no intention of giving it by half-
measures.
However, we must add that this acceptance of the proposed debate 'in a moment of foolishness' is no ironical
paradox. In reality, this gives Paul the opportunity of
meditating once more on his apostolic experience; of looking back over his whole life and of presenting it in a very
objective, very realistic light, hiding neither its greatness
nor its weakness. In doing this Paul is irresistibly led to
bring out the work of God in his life, the marvels of grace
he received, the hand of God directing the whole of his
extraordinary existence. This testimony of his whole life,
given in a 'moment of foolishness', will reveal the greatest homage to the Wisdom of God alone.

'But wherein any man is bold – I am speaking foolishly
– I also am bold. Are they Hebrews? So am I. Are they
offspring of Abraham? So am I. Are they Israelites?
So am I.
Are they ministers of Christ? I – to speak as a fool – am
more: in many more labours, in prisons more frequent-
ly, in lashes above measure (...). In labor and hardships, in many sleepless nights, in hunger and thirst, in
fastings often, in cold and nakedness. Besides those outer
things there is my daily pressing anxiety, the care of
all the churches. Who is weak, and I am not weak. Who
is made to stumble and I am not inflamed?'

                                                (11, 21-29)

Paul possesses all the titles of which any man can boast
on the religious plane. They contrast Judaising preachers
with him: but isn't he as purely Jewish as any one? They
boost his adversaries as great servants of Christ; but in
this domain, who can claim to be better than he? If they
judge an Apostle from the number of trials endured for the

Name of Christ *(cf. Ac. 5, 41)*, no one else has endured more than he; if they judge him from the sense of his responsibility, who else but Paul has received a universal mission to all the nations? Who else can boast of taking the effective part that he, Paul, has been taking for years in the life of the whole Church – and in the life of even the poorest Christian?

Paul is carried away by his passion; he no longer discusses, he affirms, he throws the witness of his life in the face of his contradictors. All that is needed to convince them that he is a real. Apostle, is to examine his way of life, to see him, to hear him. Doesn't everything about him proclaim to all that he is the Apostle of Christ and that only? Can they still be heedless enough – or malevolent enough – to compare with him so-called apostles, doubtful characters whose show of zeal is often merely external? Cannot they recognise that Paul is the envoy of Christ from all the wonderful signs of his daily life that proclaim him so?

Yet, however:

'If I must boast, I will boast of the things that concern my weakness.

The God and Father of the Lord Jesus, who is blessed forevermore, knows that I do not lie. In Damascus, the governor under King Aretas was guarding the city of the Damascenes in order to arrest me, but I was lowered in a basket through a window in the wall, and escaped his hands.'   *(11, 30-33)*

What does the recalling of this strange episode signify? Why introduce this dramatic souvenir into a page so vibrant with emotion? Paul himself explains: 'If I must boast, I will boast of the things that concern my weakness...'. His weakness as a man! It appears, in truth, in this incident at Damascus. For, in all the other trials he has just enumerated, if he revealed himself weak, because subject to suffering and persecution, he also revealed himself strong, since he was able to endure them and at last to overcome them. Now he, Paul, unlike so many others, wants to boast only of what reveals his insufficiency and incapacity, his inability to do anything without the help of God. His flight from Damascus makes this evident: here it is quite obvious that only the merciful intervention of God saved him from imminent danger for the sole purpose of retaining him in the Lord's service. Throughout his career, Paul wants to stress this one outstanding feature, the luminous revelation of the grace of God in the weakness of man, is an ideal lesson for all boasters. Therefore let man seek his glory in God, in God alone, or in his own weakness as man, to take the other side of the same truth.

'If I must boast – it is not indeed expedient to do so – but I will come to visions and revelations of the Lord. I know a man in Christ who fourteen years ago – whether in the body I do not know, or out of the body I do not know, God knows – such a one was caught up to the third heaven. And I know such a man – whether in the body or out of the body I do not know, God knows – that he was caught up into paradise and heard secret words that man may not repeat.' (*12, 1-4*)

That man is evidently Paul himself. He was favoured with an absolutely unique mystical grace, the highest imaginable. He received from the Lord Himself revelations so great that all the spiritually gifted persons in Corinth seemed non-existent compared to him. He would therefore have a right to argue that these exceptional graces should make the Corinthians, so inexperienced in mystic phenomena, recognise his authority. For 'of such a man' he might legitimately boast.
But Paul does not want them to see such a man in him; there is in him another man, the only one he wants to know and of whom he wishes to glory:

'But of myself, I will glory in nothing save in my infirmities.' (*12, 5*)

What a paradox! To refuse to draw glory, honour, authority, from the highest and most authentic mystical favours
– which Paul evaluates at their true worth – to bring out
only his weakness as man! This example of simplicity, of
total humility, given by the founder and master to his
disciples, who had become too self-sufficient, is an ironic
answer to the pretensions of the Corinthians. Spiritual
pride, the most subtle of all, is here irrevocably condemned.

But where did Paul make this extraordinary discovery of
the greatness of weakness? Flesh and blood did not teach
it to him; man's wisdom did not initiate him. God Himself
imposed upon him an extremely painful experience, which
made him see into the mystery of weakness.

> '(...) There was given me a thorn for the flesh, a mes-
> senger of Satan, to buffet me. Concerning this I thrice
> besought the Lord that it might leave me. And he has
> said to me 'My grace is sufficient for thee, for strength
> is made perfect in weakness.'
> (12, 7-9)

What a contrast with the mystic graces, the visions, the
revelations, the catching up to the third heaven! God willed
this striking contrast in Paul's experience in order to make
him fully His witness. This thorn in the flesh is very probably the chronic illness to which we have alluded already
in this *Letter*. It is a hard trial, moral as much as physical; its painful attacks reduced Paul to total inaction and
plunged him into a profound prostration. In these temporary prostrations of his whole being, Paul was able to
learn what God wanted him to learn; the nothingness of
man – the all-powerfulness of the grace of God. He learned
it – oh! not spontaneously, for his natural reaction as man,
and even as a believer, was to ask his deliverance from
the Lord; he did ask it 'three times', that means with all
the insistence that a man in agony can put into his
prayer: the insistence of Christ Himself in the Garden of
Olives... He was not heard. For him God reserved a still
higher grace: the discovery of strength in weakness. For

the strength of God is revealed, with incomparable brilliance in the weakness of His servants. It is more than revealed: according to the real sense of the Greek verb used by Paul, it is perfected, it is completed, it is apprehended in human weakness 'to show that the abundance of the power is God's and not ours' *(4, 7)*. This is an unforgettable discovery, which gave Paul an entirely new insight into the world and into his own life. It is a sense of the Christian paradox, which opened to him the mysterious avenues of the Wisdom of God. The former Pharisee became the witness of the efficacy of grace alone.

> 'Gladly therefore I will glory in my infirmities, that the strength of Christ may dwell in me. Wherefore I am satisfied, for Christ's sake, with infirmities, with insults, with hardships, with persecutions, with distresses. For when I am weak, then I am strong.' *(12, 9-10)*

As we have said, Paul discovered this mystery of weakness in his own experience. But was experience enough? No, it could only teach him what Christ had revealed to him. It would have taught him nothing if he had not had the light of Christ: the light which comes from the Cross and the Resurrection. Hence apostolic experience, a completion of the Christian experience, is consummated in the Mystery of Christ and of our insertion in Him:

> 'For though he was crucified through weakness, yet he lives through the power of God. Yes, we also are weak in him, yet we shall live with him through the power of God in your regard.' *(13, 4)*

Weakness and humility of Christ nailed to the Cross, and of our humanity crucified with Him; strength, greatness and glory of the risen Christ, and of our resurrection in Him: there is what gives sense and meaning to the testimony, at once painful and triumphant, that Paul left us in this *Second Letter to the Corinthians.*

4

Christ Our Only Salvation

The Letter to the Galatians

The Galatians were Celts from Asia, who, about the year 530 B.C., had entered the centre and west of Europe, especially Gaul. By the middle of the fourth century, they had advanced to Greece, and had gone from there to Asia Minor.

In the time of Saint Paul, they held, in the centre of Asia Minor, territory formed from an irregular strip of land, going from north to south. The territory of the real native Galatians was the northern part of this strip of land around Ancyrus; the southern part was formed from annexments and enlargements conceded by Rome for services rendered. The whole formed the Roman province of Galatia. We know from the *Acts of the Apostles* that Paul, in the course of his first missionary journey (Ac. 13, 14), evangelised Antioch in Pisidia, Lystra, Iconium, Derbe, all Galatian towns, but in the southern part of this province. Is it to these communities that the *Letter to the Galatians* is addressed? We would, at first sight, be tempted to think so. But would Paul not have had the opportunity of founding Churches more to the north, among the real Galatians? Indeed on two different occasions, during his second and third missionary journeys, the Book of the Acts mentions that Paul passed 'through the Galatian country *(Ac. 16, 6, and 18, 23)*. This term, coupled with the journey indicated, at least in the first of these texts, would suggest rather the northern part of Galatia, the country of the real Galatians. To be exact, Paul, in his *Letter,* calls his correspondents 'Galatians' (3, 1). So we have reasons for thinking that it is to the communities of northern Galatia that Paul wrote this *Letter*.

Under these conditions, the *Letter to the Galatians* can date only from the third missionary journey. Paul, after having visited these Churches (Ac. 18, 23), stays in Ephesus; there he receives disquieting news: Judaising propaganda was disseminated in the communities immediately after his departure. He has to intervene without delay. Therefore he writes this *Letter*, either in Ephesus, or in Corinth, where he stays immediately afterwards (Ac. 20, 3).

So the *Letter to the Galatians* was written about the same time as the great *Epistle to the Romans*. This means that relationship of themes and resemblances of style in both are striking. It is probable that the *Letter to the Galatians* was written first, undoubtedly in the year 56 A.D.

Its authenticity has scarcely ever been discussed. It is, we can say, the most 'Pauline' of all the *Epistles* of Saint Paul.

A. – *The apostolic vocation*

What a difference between the beginning of the *Letter to the Galatians* and that of Paul's other *Letters*! Here, neither congratulations, nor giving of thanks, nor paternal insistence on union in prayer... But from the first words, an explosion of almost unrestrained violence:

'Paul, an Apostle, sent not from men nor by man, but by Jesus Christ and God the Father...'   *(1, 1)*

Paul's intention is clear enough! He wants to take up a position immediately on a litigious point. This is none other than the question of his right to the title of Apostle. In the Galatian communities, Paul's enemies had sown doubts about this. Of Peter, James, and those whom Jesus had chosen during His earthly life, they could be sure; they were indeed authentically Apostles. But that fellow Paul, what did anyone know about his vocation? What did it mean? By what authority was it recognised? Besides, his doctrine seemed a little too personal. Was he in agreement with the mother-Church in Jerusalem? Was he an authentic envoy of Christ? Thus, both Paul's person and his message were questioned.

He was not a man to leave such attacks unanswered. With all the energy of his character and all the conviction of his conscience, he will focalise everything necessary. In doing so, he will give us one of the most important testimonies we have to the authenticity of his vocation, as well as the most impassioned and the most vigorous explanation of his message, or, as he says himself, his 'Gospel'.

'Paul, an Apostle, sent not from men nor by man but by Jesus Christ...' This definition is of paramount importance. Paul proclaims himself an apostle possessing the same title as the Twelve whom Jesus had chosen, the same title as Peter to whom they wished to oppose him. He holds his apostolic vocation directly from Jesus himself; therefore he speaks not with a man's authority but with the Lord's. He was not like Barnabas or Silas sent by man.

Now that recalls other vocations, familiar to readers of the Bible, the vocations of the Prophets. Does not Paul stand in the same position with regard to Christ, as the Prophets of the Old Testament with regard to God? When he so vigorously denies that his vocation has a human origin, we recognise the energy with which the Prophets reiterated the same denial to their enemies:

> 'I am not a prophet nor am I the son of a prophet; but I am a herdsman plucking wild figs. And the Lord took me when I followed the flock, and the Lord said to me: Go, prophecy to my people Israel.' (*Am. 7, 14-15*)

answered Amos to the high-priest of Bethel, who wanted to prevent him from speaking. Amos was truly a prophet and was fully conscious of speaking as such. But he absolutely refused to be classified in the same fraternity as the prophets-by-profession types well known in Israel at that time. He proclaimed that his vocation had its source in the direct intervention of God in his life.

The same implicit affirmation is found in all the accounts of prophetic vocations in the Old Testament. Whether it be Moses, or Isaiah, or Jeremias, or Ezechiel, all have left us the witness of a direct meeting with God, Who independently of any human intervention, chose them to become His heralds among men.

In Paul's case this non-human origin of his vocation is revealed, with startling evidence, in the total break which marked his life.

> 'For you have heard of my former manner of life in Judaism; how beyond all measure I persecuted the Church of God, and ravaged it. And I advanced in Judaism above many of my contemporaries in my nation, showing much more zeal for the tradition of my fathers. But when it pleased him who from my mother's womb set me apart and called me by His grace, to reveal his Son in me, that I might preach Him among the Gentiles, immediately, without taking counsel with flesh and blood, and without going up to Jerusalem, to those who were appointed apostles before me, I retired...'
>
> *(I, 13-17)*

This complete change in Paul is not only a conversion; it is the manifest proof of divine intervention, because it was humanly unthinkable and remains humanly inexplicable. Paul is absolutely opposed to our seeking to analyse the psychological process which could have preceded, and, in some way, prepared this change of front. In that also, he is of one mind with the Prophets. Nothing indeed is more foreign to the prophetic conscience than the idea of a psychological preparation for one's vocation. Neither ascetic discipline nor mystic ascent, by purification of the senses or the mind, gives a person the dispositions for this meeting with God. Whoever seeks to define the stages of such a preparation, not only constructs a gratuitous supposition but deviates radically from the viewpoints of Prophetic theology. In fact, for the Prophet, his seizure by God is always completely new, divine intervention being, both in the life of man and in world history, always essentially creative.

We speak of being made completely new. From man's

point of view this is indeed a fact. But is it so when we look at it in the eternal Design of God?

To this question, the Prophets have already answered:

'Before I formed thee in the Bowels of thy mother, I knew thee: and before thou camest forth out of the womb, I sanctified thee,'   (Jer. 1, 5)

we read in the vocation of Jeremias.

'The Lord hath called me from the womb: from the bowels of my mother He hath been mindful of my name,'   (Is. 49, 1)

says the Servant of God to us, resuming the testimony of Jeremias himself.

Besides, Paul expresses the same consciousness of his vocation, in terms which he borrows from these two Prophets. To the newness created in his life by the divine intervention, he opposes the eternal choice of God. Like the Prophets, the Apostle has the loftiest consciousness of the greatness of his vocation. He knows that he is playing an indispensable part in the working out of God's plan in the world. Indispensable, not, of course, by reason of its personal human value, but by reason of a free and eternal decision of God.

The consciousness of this eternal choice, the certainty of His call are such that all recourse to an earthly authority, whatever it be, becomes superfluous. For the Apostle, as for the Prophet, the authority of God, Who calls him is of itself sufficient. When he hears the divine Word, there is no need of human authentication. That is why Paul tells us that he has not consulted flesh and blood, that he did not go up to Jerusalem to those who were apostles before him. Let us not see in that a sort of bravado intended for those who were discussing his right to the title of apostle. The affirmation, of course, is directed against them; but it expresses above all the profound consciousness of his vocation.

Consciousness of his vocation is what Paul expresses when he tells us:

> 'For I give you to understand, brethren, that the gospel which was preached by me is not of man. For I did not receive it from man, nor was I taught it; but I received it by a revelation of Jesus Christ.' (1, 11)

Paul often uses this expression 'not of man'. It evokes all that belongs to the limited sphere of man, of his intelligence, his designs, his actions. So Paul affirms that his message is of quite a different order from that which men think or imagine. It is not a human teaching, like that which our Lord accused the Pharisees of imposing on Israel (Mk. 7, 7-13)

If it is not such, it has no human origin. 'For I did not receive it from man, nor was I taught it...' Paul says to us. Yet we must understand this declaration. Let us not think that Paul claims to have learned everything by one immediate direct revelation of the Lord. In reality, we guess from his Letters that he had many contacts with the Tradition of the apostolic Community. What more normal, anyhow? At the time of his conversion, he certainly received Christian instruction, of the contemporary catechetical type. After that, in his contacts with the disciples and the Apostles, at Damascus, Antioch and Jerusalem, he had many opportunities of receiving instruction on Jesus, on His life and His message. Surely he learned much in that way.

Moreover, why would Paul have wanted to set his knowledge of Christ against the tradition of the apostolic Community? Nothing is more profoundly biblical than the idea of tradition; the Prophets themselves bear witness to this. Steeped as he was in biblical revelation and in the Jewish mentality, how could Paul have denied the worth of Tradition in the Christian Church, the continuation of the Israel of the Old Testament.

If he tells us that he has learned his 'Gospel' from no human master, let us understand him thoroughly. His 'Gospel' does not designate here the totality of the catechetics which he was teaching, but only what constitutes the originality of the Pauline doctrine: the abolition by Christ of the regime of the Law. That is exactly the subject of this *Letter* and the cause of all the difficulties in the Churches of Galatia:

> 'But even if we or an angel from heaven should preach a gospel to you other than that which we have preached to you,' *cries out Paul*, 'let him be anathema!'   *(1, 8)*

His message is not a message that is different in all respects, but only in one respect of paramount importance, that is the relation between faith in Christ and the regime of the Law.

This Gospel, this message of the abolition of the Law by Christ, Paul did not learn from any man. The hellenistic group of the Jerusalem community had undoubtedly prepared for it; at any rate that is the chief accusation of the Jews against Stephen *(Ac. 7, 13-14)*. But it is Paul who really elaborated this doctrine and made of it the very basis of his preaching. In this sense, he had his own Gospel. And if he tells us that he received it through a revelation of Jesus Christ, he is undoubtedly alluding to the vision on the road to Damascus. The Galatians undoubtedly knew all about this event. On that day, Paul became conscious of his apostolic mission, and aware that the way of salvation lay through Christ alone independently of the Law. He is right. Did he not on that day experience the all-powerfulness of the risen Christ? His Gospel is but the development of this knowledge of Jesus in 'the power of His resurrection' *(Phil. 13, 10)*

B. – *Paul's mission in the Church*

However absolutely Paul affirmed the supernatural origin and the independence of his mission, nevertheless, on two different occasions, he wanted to go to Jerusalem. The first time was three years after his conversion.

'Then after three years I went to Jerusalem to see Peter, and I remained with him fifteen days. But I saw none of the other apostles, except James, the brother of the Lord.' *(1, 18-19)*

Paul stresses the private character and the limited significance of this first step. However it constitutes a recognition of at least the moral authority of Peter. But Paul's second step will be much more important.

'Then after fourteen years I went up again to Jerusalem with Barnabas, taking also Titus along with me. And I went up in consequence of a revelation, I conferred with them on the Gospel which I preach among the Gentiles, but separately with the men of authority; lest perhaps I should be running or had run in vain.' *(2, 1-2)*

Unlike the first, this is no longer a private but an official visit. Paul undertakes it in consequence of an express manifestation of the will of the Lord. He takes Barnabas and Titus with him; the composition of the group indicates sufficiently well that the most notable representatives of the Church of Antioch accompany him on this official visit to the Jerusalem community.

The significance of such a step is of paramount importance for the understanding of Paul's soul. It reveals his comprehension of the hierarchical Church which, up to this, he had no opportunity of evincing. Paul did not claim to dissociate his personal mission from the authority of the mother-Church in Jerusalem. He who has just proclaimed Christ his sole Master, the immediate and direct author of his vocation and his mission, wishes to have the authenticity of his message recognised by Peter, James and John. Undoubtedly this step was imposed by the difficulties of the moment, and its mention in the *Letter to the Galatians* has an apologetic value for Paul. None the less it remains the witness of an ecclesial preoccupation, which is very interesting to note in a man as independent and as sure of his vocation as Paul was. Because we can be certain that he never really doubted the worth of his work nor the authenticity of his Gospel. Consequently the step he takes in going to Jerusalem becomes more interesting still.

Besides this visit to Jerusalem shows clearly the essential agreement between Paul and the other Apostles. He delights in stressing this for the benefit of his detractors:

> 'On the contrary, when they saw that to me was committed the gospel for the uncircumcised, as to Peter that for the circumcised (for he who worked in Peter for the apostleship of the circumcised worked also in me among the Gentiles) – and when they recognised the grace that was given to me, James and Cephas and John, who were considered the pillars, gave to me and to Barnabas the right hand of fellowship, that we should go to the Gentiles, and they to the circumcised: provided only that we should be mindful of the poor, the very thing I was eager to do.' *(2, 7-10)*

Paul insists here, as in the *Letter to the Galatians,* on a collection in favour of the poor of Jerusalem. He saw more in this than a mere charitable gesture; for him, this collection was a sign of the unity of the Church of Christ itself. Hence he assigned to it great importance. It bore witness to the fact that the young communities of the Roman world were true sons of the mother-Church in Jerusalem. In such a humble and apparently so material a preoccupation, we still perceive Paul's comprehension of the Church.

After the complete agreement manifested at the meeting in Jerusalem, we can understand the incident at Antioch.

> 'But when Cephas came to Antioch, I withstood him to his face, because he was deserving of blame. For before certain persons came from James, he used to eat with the Gentiles; but when they came, he began to withdraw and to separate himself, fearing the circumcised. And the rest of the Jews dissembled along with

him, so that Barnabas also was led away by them into that dissimulation.

But when I saw that they were not walking uprightly according to the truth of the Gospel, I said to Cephas before them all: If thou, though a Jew, livest like the Gentiles, and not like the Jews, how is it that thou dost compel the Gentiles to live like the Jews?' *(2, 11-14)*

We can understand the embarrassing situation in which Peter found himself. He comes to Antioch, becomes acquainted with converted Gentiles and decides to take his meals with them, thus revoking the rules of alimentary purity in Judaism. But now, Christians of Jewish origin from James's entourage, i.e. from an environment particularly attached to the retaining of Jewish customs, within Christianity, arrive in Antioch. Did they reproach Peter? He, for his part, thinks it his duty to manage them, and, from that day, withdraws from the Gentile Christians.

We can guess how troubled and humiliated these were. Paul, their Apostle, reacts vigorously. He reprimands Peter for his inconsistency: after having abandoned Jewish customs he goes back to them! Such an attitude can only sow discord among the Gentile Christians: they will think themselves obliged to submit to the regulation of the Jewish Law, if they want to be fully accepted by their brothers in the Church of Christ. For Paul, this position is inadmissible. He realises, more than any other Apostle of this time, that the Coming of Christ marks the end of the Law. His opposition to Peter in this circumstance reveals, not that he denied his authority – on the contrary, the incident presupposes that Peter's authority was recognised by all – but that he understood more clearly than he the relations of the Christian faith with Judaism.

This understanding he wished to share with all. He expresses it, even here, in a little discourse which one would imagine was addressed to Peter but which is in reality a synthesis of 'his Gospel' intended for the Galatians. Its last words make clear its whole sense and admirably summarise Paul's whole message:

> 'I do not cast away the grace of God. For if justice is
> by the Law, then Christ died in vain.'   *(2, 21)*

In this we have the strongest, most definite expression of
Paul's theological thought. All his efforts as a Christian
thinker tended towards one object: to put in its proper
place and to shed full light upon the grace of God. Now he
understood that the grace of God, which contains in itself
the whole work of salvation, has henceforth a precise
meaning: it designates the gratuitous justice that God
grants us through Christ. To seek another principle of
justice – the Law – is therefore going contrary to the grace
of God, reducing Christ to a secondary role in the work of
salvation, giving to the Cross a purely accessory value.
The Mystery of Christ is henceforth all; to claim to add
anything at all to it is to reduce it to nothing and to go
against the only valid knowledge of the Design of God.
Paul's mission was to ensure the triumph of this 'Gospel
message' in the Church.

C. – *Law and faith*

Paul is a logician. He is not content with affirming; he
wants to convince. Hence he engages in a passionate debate with the Galatians about Christ and the Law. They
fought his teaching; he will defend himself as he knows
how, by counter-attacking with all his energy, with all his
ardour, all his knowledge also. The disciple of Gamaliel is
unembarrassed in these theological discussions. He is so
much at ease in them that we often experience some difficulty in following him. Once we accept his viewpoints we
assimilate his very enriching thought.

Paul first appeals to the Galatians' own experience:

> 'This only I would learn from you: Did you receive the
> Spirit in virtue of the works of the Law, or in virtue of
> hearing and believing?'   *(3, 2)*

We know from the *Book of the Acts* and from Paul's own *Letters* that the Pauline Churches were very spiritually gifted, as were most of the Christian communities in the Primitive Church. The Galatians had also experienced the gifts of the Spirit and the miracles which accompanied them. Their community had had its Pentecost; it had had the sensible certainty of possessing the Gift of God, the Spirit, promised by the Prophet for the Messianic times. But when had they had this experience? At their Baptism, on their entrance into the Church of Christ. So they did not owe the Spirit to the practice of the Law, but to an act of faith in Christ.

So the Galatians know that they have embarked on the Messianic era. But in their Christian faith they would like to include the observation of the Jewish Law. How is it that they do not realise that this is a retrograde step? The order of God's plan is to lead from preparation to completion, from the Law to Faith, from the 'flesh', i.e. external[1] religious observance, to the Spirit, to a religion animated from inside by the Spirit of God Himself, as the Prophets Jeremias and Ezechiel had proclaimed *(Jer. 31, 33; Ez. 11, 19-20; 36, 26-27)*. The poor Galatians want to upset this divine Plan; they do not understand it at all. Very well! Let us show them now by Holy Scripture, the Word of God Himself, that Salvation comes by faith alone.

For we read in the book of Genesis:

> 'Abraham believed God, and it was credited to him as justice.' *(3, 6; cf. Gen. 15, 6)*

and again:

> 'In thee shall all the nations be blessed.'
> *(3, 8; cf. Gen. 12, 3 & 18, 18)*

So if we wish to share in the universal benediction

Author's Note: 1. Here, the expression 'the flesh' probably contains an allusion to circumcision.

promised to Abraham, we must imitate him in his faith alone. On this condition we shall be truly sons of Abraham.

'If you are the children of Abraham do the works of Abraham.' *(Jn. 8, 39)*

Abraham had no need of the practice of the Law to be justified: he did not know it! God justified him in sole consideration of his faith.
Moreover, can the Law itself justify man? We read in Deuteronomy this terrible threat:

'Cursed is everyone who does not hold to all things that are written in the book of the Law.' *(3, 10; cf. Dt. 27, 26)*

Now it is humanly impossible to observe the Law without failing sometimes! Paul learned this sufficiently well in his experience as a Pharisee, and Peter, for his part, spoke to the council of Jerusalem about 'this yoke which neither our fathers nor we have been able to bear' *(Ac. 15, 10)*. Scripture teaches us that man is too weak to be always faithful, without any fault, to the will of God.
Then, by a sort of cruel irony, the man who is expecting justification from the practice of the Law falls inevitably under the lash of the malediction of this same Law! And the benediction promised to the man who will observe it perfectly, evades him always.
It is only in Abraham that man can attain the divine benediction, source of all good. By our act of faith, we are inserted in Christ, who took upon Himself the divine malediction merited by our faults, and we thus inherit the benediction of Abraham.
Because, let us be sure of it, this promise made to Abraham remains always valid. The Law has not annulled it. Paul, who will always love juridical comparisons, real parables in which he will illustrate his teaching, like our Lord in the parables of the Gospel, invokes a very simple example: nobody can modify, still less annul, a will or testament drawn up in good or due form. Very well! God

drew up a real testament in favour of Abraham and of his offspring, because, let us not forget, the same Greek word signifies 'testament' and 'covenant'. Paul plays on this double meaning as he will do later in his *Epistle to the Hebrews*. The content of this testament, of this covenant, was the Messianic Promise. Through Abraham it pointed at Christ: and Paul with a typical rabbinic subtlety even guesses allusion to Christ in the text of Genesis 'your Offspring', in the singular, and not, as one would expect, 'your offsprings', (the plural) which would have pointed at the Israelites. Christ is therefore Abraham's heir, and with Him all those who will believe in Him. The Law which appeared only several centuries after this first Covenant, was unable to invalidate it.

Of course, we could object to Paul that the same God being the author of the testament and the Law, could want to replace the first by the second. But Paul is not embarrassed by such considerations. His parable, like every parable, is incomplete and open to discussion, if we want to apply it in all its details. The only point which really matters is the intangibility of the testament. Paul saw in it a beautiful image of the constant doctrine of the Bible: the faithfulness of God to His promise.

But then, we can ask ourselves a question: what is the meaning of the Mosaic Law? Why was it given to Israel if the Promise is definitely the only reality which counts in the plan of God? Does not Paul take away all value from this Law of Sinai, an arrangement superadded after a thrust had been made at the Promise, a superfluous element, and even, by a cruel paradox, a cause of malediction for mankind?

Paul asked himself this essential question. He answers it in one incisive sentence

'The Law was enacted on account of transgressions until the offspring should come to whom the promise was made.' *(3, 19)*

On account of transgressions... The ancient theologians
wished it to mean: *to put down transgressions*. But Paul's
real thought leaves no doubt. He means: to provoke and
multiply the transgressions against the Divine will. He
will express himself very clearly in the *Letter to the
Romans:*

'The Law intervened that the offence might abound.'
(*Rom.* 5, 20)

How understand such a paradoxical affirmation? God
would have given a Law that offences might abound?
Yes, and this idea, at first inacceptable, almost scandal-
ous, is very beautiful and very lofty. What Paul means to
bring out fully, is that salvation comes solely by the grace
of God which is given us in Christ. Grace of God, i.e. total,
absolute gratuity. Now, there is no more absolute gratuity
than that of pardon. Since the coming of Christ, the multiplication of faults serves as a manifestation, so much the
more striking, of grace, since it permits God to display
all the riches of His pardon. Hence sin becomes a positive
value in the plan of God. As Saint Augustine, the great disciple of Saint Paul will say later, sin also concurs in the
work of the salvation of mankind. There is no further need
to be scandalised at the fact that the Law was enacted 'on
account of transgressions'. Because these transgressions
prepared the triumph of the grace of God in the coming of
Christ. No man, neither Jew nor Gentile, can boast of
owing his salvation to his own merits. The infinite grace
of Christ, of which we become beneficiaries by faith, is the
sole source of universal salvation. Such is the eternal will
of God. The Old Testament itself reveals it to us, by in-
sisting so often on the sin of mankind:

'But the Scripture shut up all things under sin, that by
the faith of Jesus Christ the promise might be given to
those who believe.'   (*3, 22*)

Therefore the Law has had a very great role. But a temporary role by definition. Ordered to the striking manifestation of the grace of God, it has but to disappear when this grace is revealed, with the coming of Christ.

'The Law has been our tutor unto Christ.'   *(3, 24)*

The tutor, in the society of Paul's time is not always a teacher. In the families of the well-to-do he is merely a slave, charged with taking the child to school and, in general, with superintending him. Paul is thinking only of this role of tutor. A transitory role, since it ceases when the child becomes a man. A role of constraint, since it regulates and superintends the child's conduct.

Such was the role of the Law. We were 'shut up under the Law' until the messianic time, the time of Faith. Now that the faith is revealed to us, we have no longer anything to do with the Law; its role is ended. We have reached the majority of the sons of God, all we who have received baptism in which our act of faith in Christ is fully realised. What further need have we of a preceptor, of a guardian. We have been inserted in Christ; Whatever be our race or social origin, we are all one in Christ. With Him we are then this offspring of Abraham who must inherit the Promise. The time of Christ, i.e. our time, is far superior to the time of the Law, no less than to the time of the Promise and the Faith in which Abraham lived.

We are therefore by faith, heirs of the Promise. And here is a new parable, still juridical, which will permit us to understand better the religious history of humanity, our own history.

'As long as the heir is a child, he differs in no way from a slave, though he is the master of all; but he is under guardians and stewards until the time set by his father. So we too, when we were children, were enslaved under the elements of the world. But when the fullness of time came, God sent his Son, born of a woman, born under the Law, that he might redeem those who were under the Law, that we might receive the adoption of sons.'

(4, 1-6)

The history of mankind is divided into two epochs; the first is that of slavery: man is a slave of 'the elements of the world', not the four elements, of which Paul is evidently not thinking here, but the Law, an elementary and earthly teaching compared to that of Christ. However this slave is the Son of God; he is called to reign over the universe. When man lost this lordship, received at the moment of His creation, and fell into servitude, God decided to redeem him. Apparently absent from the history of man, God really guides it completely. History has a meaning, because it has an end which will explain all its evolutions.

This end is Christ, who is the spiritual fullness of the human race. The Son of God, willed to share our weakness as men who were under the guardianship of the Law. But this slavery, freely accepted, has for that very reason, redemptive value. The Son of God took our place by means of His Incarnation and Sacrifice. As a result we were able to have access to this title of sonship, to which we were called, thus becoming heirs of the new creation, we who had lost our original lordship over the first creation of God.

That we are sons we know well. Have we not the Spirit of Jesus in us? Once more, Paul appeals to the religious experience of his Galatians. How could they who have received the Spirit return to carnal 'elements'? The presence of the Spirit in the Church testifies to the fullness of time and to the disappearance of the limited regime of the Law.

D. – *Sara and Agar Slavery or Liberty*

'You who desire to be under the Law, have you not read the Law? For it is written that Abraham had two sons, the one by a slave-girl and the other by a free woman.'

(4, 21-22)

The Galatians are tempted to submit to the Jewish Law. Very well. In this same Law, Paul will find an argument against them. He will invoke the Law against the Law. The word Law includes, in fact, several very different realities. The Law can be the ritual regulation of Judaism; as such, it is abolished by Christ. But the Law is also the revelation, the Word of God. Now, the Word of God 'endureth forever' (Is. 40, 8). That is why Paul can invoke the Law against itself. He invokes the authority of the Divine Word against Jewish legalism.

Now what does the Law, the Word of God say to us? We read, in *Genesis,* first of the five books of the Law, that Abraham had a child Ismael by his slave Agar. Later, occurred the marvellous birth of Sara's child, Isaac. In these two women, Paul to whom the allegoric exegesis of the rabbis was familiar, recognises the symbol of the two Covenants. Agar, from whom the Arabs descended through Ismael, evokes Sinai, situated in the approaches to Arabia; she therefore represents very well the First Covenant, concluded by Moses. Thus the first Covenant is a regime of slavery. But Sara, the free woman, evokes the heavenly Jerusalem i.e. the Church to which we belong. We are therefore free, free with respect to the Law, with respect to every earthly reality, none of which can now reduce us to slavery.

'But as then he who was born according to the flesh persecuted him who was born according to the spirit, so also it is now. But what does the Scripture say? 'Cast out the slave-girl and her son, for the son of the slave-girl shall not be heir with the son of the free woman'.'
(4, 29-30 cf. Gen. 21, 10)

We must not be scandalised if the Church meets with persecution; Isaac, the child of the free woman, the child of the Promise, was indeed persecuted by the slave's son. Our history is already mysteriously written in these first pages of the Bible. But the denouement of this history is written also, for those readers with the insight of faith.

176

And this denouement gives us hope: the heavenly inheritance, promised to Abraham, is reserved for us, for us his true offspring who live not in the slavery of the Law, but in the liberty of Faith.

Let us not be astonished at this Pauline interpretation of the history of Isaac and Ismael. It is not explained solely, by the contemporary popular taste for allegory. It expresses a profound truth: henceforth, the Christian reads the Bible in the light of Christ; he must be able to recognise in it the gradual revelation of Christ. This is not a fantastic interpretation, but a re-reading from a new point of view. Paul who discovered interior liberty on discovering Christ can recognise in the Law, proclamations, until then veiled, concerning the liberty of believers.

Let us not think that he wanted 'to lay hold of' the Galatians by a well-known feature of their character: the taste for independence, common to their race. It is not a question here of independence but of liberty, which is quite a different matter. It is not a question of a psychological characteristic, but of a marvellous spiritual discovery, of the very experience that Paul had when he was 'laid hold of' by Christ Jesus (Phil. 3, 12).

Real liberty! Paul will finish its definition for us.

> 'For you have been called to liberty, brethren; only do not use liberty as an occasion for sensuality, but by charity serve one another.' *(5, 13)*

It is so easy to be equivocal on the word liberty! Moreover, the human race has never failed to be equivocal. In all epochs of the Church's history, Christians are found who, in the name of sham spiritual liberty, give themselves up to serious laxity. As early as the time of Saint Paul, this danger was becoming evident. He is to return vigorously to this subject in his *Letter to the Romans (6, 15)*. Saint Peter, for his part, will address an energetic warning to the Christians:

'Live as freemen, yet not using your freedom as a cloak for malice.'
                                                            (I Pet. 2, 16)

The 'flesh' indeed is always ready to speak. The flesh, that is to say, that which is most fundamentally material- istic in us! In short, our egoism, our instinctive desire for ease and enjoyment. But authentic liberty has its sign, by which it is recognised: charity. It puts us at the service of our brothers, after the example of Christ, Who did not come to be served, but to serve. It makes us accept the sacrifices required by life in a fraternal community.

The whole paradox of Christian liberty lies there. It makes servants of us, servants of our brothers, and by that very fact servants of God, since His entire Law is summed up in this single commandment: 'Thou shalt love thy neighbour as thyself'.

Christian liberty is not facility but requirement. It asks man to forget himself to give himself to God and to his brothers. Solely at this price, he will know what it is to be free.

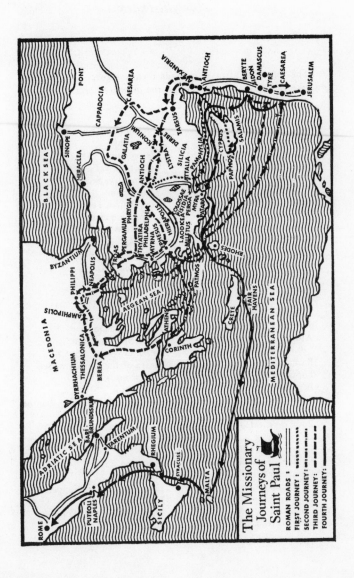

The Missionary
Journeys of
Saint Paul

ROMAN ROADS:
FIRST JOURNEY:
SECOND JOURNEY:
THIRD JOURNEY:
FOURTH JOURNEY:

Analytic Index

The letter 's' after a number means subject. The subject referred to is fully treated on the indicated and subsequent pages.